Arthur M. Cohen
EDITOR-IN-CHIEF

Florence B. Brawer
ASSOCIATE EDITOR

Portrait of the Rural Community College

Jim Killacky
Rural Community Development Specialist

James R. Valadez
North Carolina State University, Raleigh

EDITORS

Number 90, Summer 1995

JOSSEY-BASS PUBLISHERS
San Francisco

ERIC®

Clearinghouse for Community Colleges

PORTRAIT OF THE RURAL COMMUNITY COLLEGE
Jim Killacky, James R. Valadez (eds.)
New Directions for Community Colleges, no. 90
Volume XXIII, number 2
Arthur M. Cohen, Editor-in-Chief
Florence B. Brawer, Associate Editor

Microfilm copies of issues and articles are available in 16mm and 35mm, as well as microfiche in 105mm, through University Microfilms Inc., 300 North Zeeb Road, Ann Arbor, Michigan 48106-1346.

LC 85-644753   ISSN 0194-3081   ISBN 0-7879-9914-8

NEW DIRECTIONS FOR COMMUNITY COLLEGES is part of The Jossey-Bass Higher and Adult Education Series and is published quarterly by Jossey-Bass Inc., Publishers, 350 Sansome Street, San Francisco, California 94104-1342 in association with the ERIC Clearinghouse for Community Colleges. Second-class postage paid at San Francisco, California, and at additional mailing offices. POSTMASTER: Send address changes to New Directions for Community Colleges, Jossey-Bass Inc., Publishers, 350 Sansome Street, San Francisco, California 94104-1342.

SUBSCRIPTIONS for 1995 cost $49.00 for individuals and $72.00 for institutions, agencies, and libraries.

THE MATERIAL in this publication is based on work sponsored wholly or in part by the Office of Educational Research and Improvement, U.S. Department of Education, under contract number RI-93-00-2003. Its contents do not necessarily reflect the views of the Department, or any other agency of the U.S. Government.

EDITORIAL CORRESPONDENCE should be sent to the Editor-in-Chief, Arthur M. Cohen, at the ERIC Clearinghouse for Community Colleges, University of California, 3051 Moore Hall, 405 Hilgard Avenue, Los Angeles, California 90024-1521.

Cover photograph © Rene Sheret, After Image, Los Angeles, California, 1990.

Manufactured in the United States of America on Lyons Falls TCF Pathfinder Tradebook. This paper is acid-free and 100 percent totally chlorine-free.

CONTENTS

EDITORS' NOTES

We believe that rural community colleges hold great promise and potential for the future of this country and the world. We also believe that significant issues, problems, and developments are present in today's rural community colleges. These matters need to be given a voice in association with others so that collectively hope, inspiration, and insight may be available to those who toil in these vineyards. This edition of essays about rural community colleges had its genesis in March 1993 as Jim Killacky and George Baker, a professor at North Carolina State, drove very early one morning to visit a rural community college. Baker, a foremost scholar of community colleges, in response to Killacky's question about areas needing exploration said, "You know, there is not much going on in the area of rural community colleges. As you've spent your life working in rural communities, why not check it out?" A few weeks later, in a conversation with James Valadez, Killacky found a colleague with major interests in rural issues and community colleges and our collaboration was born. A proposal was made to and accepted by the editor-in-chief of *New Directions for Community Colleges,* and we now are pleased to present the result.

We view this volume as the first in a series focusing on the range of issues, problems, creative programs, and new directions confronting rural community colleges. Here we seek to give voice to a series of individual practitioners working in and with rural community colleges. Rural community colleges are at a critical juncture. On the one hand, they are ideally suited to be a much-needed catalyst in creating coalitions to address the range of problems and issues facing rural citizens. On the other hand, they are faced with increasingly complex fiscal and resource dilemmas in times of diminishing public funding at local, state, and federal levels. There are growing pressures for rural (and urban) community colleges to draw inward and stress traditional academic directions. Additionally, their ruralness and the lack of strong voices championing rural populations in the legislative and policy-making arenas can easily lead to a sense of disempowerment. Rural community colleges have significant choices to address and decisions to make as the journey of our societal transformation to an Information Age continues in full flight. We hope that the voices of colleagues in this volume may enhance senses of empowerment, and be of support as the journey proceeds.

Our nation might be described as a collection of paradoxes. For example, while individual acts of kindness and volunteerism—and individual donations—continue to increase, we seem unable to come to any consensus on the great issues of our time: health care, gun control, or prison reform to name but three. The extreme political and religious right appear to be gaining huge momentum, portending future social conflict that will make much of what has gone before seem like an afternoon tea party. Issues of diversity threaten to

1

drive us even further into polarized camps. Consider the controversy and divisiveness created over the passage of Proposition 187 in California, which denied social and educational services to illegal immigrants. Further consider this scenario: 30 percent of African-Americans, and 20 percent of Hispanics, earn well below the poverty level and live in worsening ghetto conditions. At the same time, an increasingly large elderly population demands health and security entitlements that compete for welfare and educational needs in a decreasing federal budget (Kennedy, 1993). Interest payments on the national debt now exceed what the government pays on health, science, agriculture, housing, environment, and justice. Drug and crime issues and dropout rates make for sobering and chilling realities.

Rural community colleges can provide at least part of the solution to some of these great issues. As a nation, the United States has and continues to put great stock in education as a foundation for producing a democratic society and participating citizenry. Rural community colleges, typically with a tripartite mission of community service, college transfer, and workforce preparedness, continue despite overwhelming odds to have a vital role in ensuring access to their constituents. The stories of how this is happening, how it can continue, and what the problems are in the process need to be given voice so that we can understand situations, learn from them, be inspired by them, and use them as models in our own practice.

Our way of thinking about this volume is to imagine ourselves glancing through a photograph album that provides snapshots of elements of the world of rural community colleges. We think of Chapters One through Six as primarily focusing on contextual aspects of rural community colleges. Chapters Seven through Ten offer a lens through which the reader can consider methods of addressing programmatic initiatives.

In Chapter One, we offer a brief overview of rural life in the United States, its contemporary issues, and the challenge for rural community colleges to have significant roles in addressing these issues.

In Chapter Two, John Cavan draws on over twenty years as a community college president to review the comprehensive mission of rural community colleges, the critical role of the president, the college as community catalyst, and future challenges for these institutions such as maintaining egalitarianism, restructuring higher education, and marketing their product.

In Chapter Three, Donald Reichard offers a case example and succinct analysis of the issues facing the president of a small rural community college, and discusses what one needs by way of preparation to effectively address these issues.

Michael J. Hill provides an essay in Chapter Four that focuses on the twenty-six tribal and rural community colleges in the nation and elaborates on their history, current status, and future roles in U.S. higher education.

Rosemary Gillett-Karam writes about women and minorities in rural community colleges in Chapter Five. She provides a rich rural context that underscores the challenges and difficulties to be addressed if there is to be positive change in the dilemmas facing women and minorities in rural community colleges.

In Chapter Six, Pamela MacBrayne addresses the growing phenomenon of distance learning and factors for rural community colleges in embracing this concept.

In Chapter Seven, Janice Nahra Friedel and Joel Lapin discuss the role of environmental scanning for rural community colleges. They make the case that the effective use of environmental scanning will greatly enhance programming, and community support for and visibility of the rural community college.

In Chapter Eight, Anne McNutt focuses on how the rural community college can support rural development—through a logical process of program development that analyzes challenges, discusses ways to meet them, and presents some hurdles to anticipate.

In Chapter Nine, Millicent Valek tells a story of effective community-college collaboration in addressing issues of population growth through a project that brought together local elected and appointed officials, business leaders, managers of community agencies, and school and community college personnel to develop and implement strategies for optimizing resources.

Pamela MacBrayne reports, in Chapter Ten, on a research study that addresses the motivating factors for rural adults who participate in distance education programs.

In Chapter Eleven, Elizabeth Foote of the ERIC Clearinghouse for Community Colleges offers an annotated bibliography of sources and information on rural community colleges.

We would like to give special thanks to our friend and colleague George Baker, for instigating the idea of putting together this volume; to the contributors for graciously being a part of it; to the internal and external reviewers whose comments enriched it; and to the editors at the ERIC Clearinghouse for Community Colleges, who gave us the framework to present it.

Jim Killacky
James R. Valadez
Editors

Reference

Kennedy, P. *Preparing for the Twenty-First Century*. New York: Random House, 1993.

JIM KILLACKY *is a rural community development specialist in Orono, Maine.*

JAMES R. VALADEZ *is assistant professor of higher education, adult and community college education, North Carolina State University at Raleigh.*

*Rural and urban divides need to be bridged if long-term solutions to
rural problems are to be found, and the role of the rural community
college as educational provider and community organizational leader
is central to success.*

Opening the Shutter

James R. Valadez, Jim Killacky

The state of life in the rural United States is a mixed one midway through this
final decade of the twentieth century. We have a picture of a country divided
into rural and urban components, with the two sides in conflict politically,
socially, and economically. As a specific example, North Carolina has gone
through a period of strong economic and population growth over the past two
decades. In rural areas, however, the North Carolina Rural Economic Development Center (1992) reported that for all the major indicators of economic
health—population, jobs, and income growth—urban areas grew twice as fast
as rural areas. The most persistent problem in rural North Carolina was
poverty, especially for children and the elderly. Current estimates indicate that
over 25 percent of children and elderly people live below the poverty level
(North Carolina Rural Economic Development Center, 1992).

Urban and rural residents must come to an understanding of the importance of the interrelatedness of the urban and rural segments of society. Why
should urban residents concern themselves about rural society? The answer
lies in the fact that urban areas have a stake in the future of rural life. Rural
land, labor, and resources such as timber, wilderness areas, and agriculture are
vital to urban survival, and we must understand their role and plan for their
conservation.

Rural communities face problems that seem at times overwhelming and
firmly entrenched. As an example, the state of education in rural communities, particularly the rural South, is an extraordinary challenge. Educational
attainment in rural areas continues to lag behind urban communities. One in
six rural adults lack a ninth-grade education compared to one in ten in urban
areas (North Carolina Rural Economic Development Center, 1992). Sixty-four
percent of rural adults had a high school diploma compared to 75 percent of
urban adults (North Carolina Rural Economic Development Center, 1991). In

the not-too-distant past, rural youth could count on finding entry-level jobs in manufacturing, coal mining, or logging and could expect to earn a decent wage. It is not difficult to understand that rural youth could see little benefit in pursuing their education beyond the acquisition of the skills they needed to do their jobs and function in society. A legacy of substandard schools has persisted, and the related social problems of high rates of illiteracy and under-employment continue to plague rural life.

As long as industries located assembly plants and textile mills in rural communities, rural workers managed to make a living. When these jobs began to disappear over the last two decades, however, young people could no longer count on a lifetime of work at the plant. To this day, assembly lines, food processing plants and textile mills form the core of the industrial jobs in the rural South. In rural North Carolina, manufacturing accounts for 30 percent of the jobs (North Carolina Rural Economic Development Center, 1992). However, the changing economy has forced rural communities to look at newly emerging "high tech" industries to provide jobs. High tech industries have looked at the rural South as an inviting location for many reasons, including cheap land, cheap labor, and a favorable business climate, but these industries have also viewed the lack of a skilled workforce as a deterrent to relocation. There is a strong need for rural areas to draw these industries to their communities, but in order to offer these industries a skilled workforce, rural communities must improve their schools and point the way for students to seek lifelong education.

The Commission on Small/Rural Community Colleges (Barnett, 1991) conducted a study of rural community colleges and suggested that the formation of partnerships within the communities to address social issues was a step toward solving the problems. The Commission cited the community college as an important focal point for helping communities identify needs, rally local groups, and provide workforce training. High rates of illiteracy emerged as a debilitating problem in rural communities. The commission pointed to the need for community involvement, with the community college assuming a central role.

This brings into focus the role of the community college in rural communities. The community college cannot solve all the problems of rural society, but it is in a position to provide wide-ranging support and educational services. Working in cooperation with state and federal agencies and the private sector, community colleges are poised to assume a leadership role for addressing social problems such as literacy, poverty, and education in rural communities. It seems that the latter part of the 1990s will be a critical time for decisions about rural life in the United States. Either we will continue to reproduce a society divided into the urban "haves" and the rural "have nots," or efforts will be made to promote opportunity for all and for rural people in particular. As pointed out by the Commission on Small/Rural Community Colleges (1992, p. 3), "Rural community colleges traditionally play a dominant role in the educational, cultural, and social aspects of rural life. They are often the center for rural community and economic development and the primary catalyst for improving the quality of rural life." Community colleges are the logical institution to provide postsecondary instruction in skills needed for entry-level technical positions, and to provide opportunity for students to consider baccalaureate degrees.

It is critical for community colleges to teach job skills, but—more importantly—each community college must assure that its constituents become critical thinkers, conservers of natural resources, and participants in the democratic process. This broadens the responsibility of the community college from an institution that prepares a skilled workforce into one that will instill in its students knowledge about their community and society at large, and prepare them to make informed decisions concerning their futures.

References

Barnett, L. (ed.). *Rural Workplace Literacy: Community College Partnerships.* Washington, D.C.: American Association of Community Colleges, 1991. (ED 338 300)

Commission on Small/Rural Community Colleges. *Forgotten Minorities: Rural Americans and the Colleges That Serve Them.* Washington, D.C.: American Association of Community Colleges, 1992. (ED 351 054)

North Carolina Rural Economic Development Center. *Securing the Future: Rural Development Strategies for the 1990s.* Raleigh, N.C.: Rural Economic Development Center, 1991.

North Carolina Rural Economic Development Center. *Economic and Social Trends Affecting Rural North Carolina.* Raleigh, N.C.: Rural Economic Development Center, 1992.

JAMES R. VALADEZ is assistant professor of higher education, adult and community college education, North Carolina State University at Raleigh.

JIM KILLACKY is a rural community development specialist in Orono, Maine.

The rural community college is a major factor in the life of its service area. Modern colleges and their presidents face many challenges, including the need to maintain egalitarianism and to restructure higher education to serve students' real needs.

The Comprehensive Mission of Rural Community Colleges

John Cavan

Since the passage of the Morrill Act in 1862, there has been an ongoing controversy in community education regarding the mission of community colleges: Can and should community colleges be all things to all people? In a recent article, Bogart wrote about the importance of defining an institution's mission, particularly the mission of community colleges. "It is difficult, if not impossible, to describe an American higher education institution today without focusing on its mission" (1994, p. 60).

The issue is one that rural community colleges, perhaps more so than urban community colleges, must address seriously. According to Eisner (cited in Bogart, 1994), defining the current mission of community colleges is difficult because what may be a sound mission in one state may not be so in another. In my view, the mission of a rural community college is a simple one: to meet the educational needs at every level of the service area community and to work to develop a tradition of education that includes a realization of the importance of higher education.

In urban areas, community colleges might be allowed to be more selective in what they provide the community because of other institutions and agencies that are available to provide cultural, social, and economic development services. This is not the case in a rural environment. In rural areas, the local community college is the only game in town for economic development, cultural enrichment, and higher education. How can the college constrain its mission?

When people in rural areas think of education, their first thought should be the local community college. The community college must be the locus of all educational and cultural experiences—what Harlacher and Gollattscheck

(1992) refer to as the educational maintenance organization (EMO). Granted, the community college may not be able to meet, by itself, every educational need of the community. But the community should look to the college to be the broker of educational services, whether it be literacy programs for community action agencies or continuing education programs for local physicians and other professionals. In other words, the concept of "all things to all people" is not only attainable but necessary for a rural community college.

Role of the President

It is the responsibility of the president of the community college to articulate the comprehensive mission of the rural college and to get congruency of this mission from the local board, local political entities, state legislators, faculty, and the total college community. Roueche, Baker, and Rose (1989) proclaim that if community colleges are to become the sources of educational, civic, and cultural renewal called for by the Futures Commission of the American Association of Community Colleges, the president will be the key to establishing the community in which this will occur. I could not agree more.

To create a community in which the mission can be effectively articulated, the community college president must understand the importance of institutional charisma and personality. First, there must be a congruency of mission among the entire college family, including administrators, faculty, staff, and board members. Second, the college family should be knowledgeable about the institution's history—Where have we been?—and in agreement about the future—Where are we going? Finally, the college family must understand and accept the role of the college and its niche in the community. Although we attempt to be all things to all people, we will find that the college can determine its role and its niche in the community.

All of the above create the special magic of the institutional charisma and personality. From the institutional charisma comes the Three E force that should drive all community colleges: Energy, Experience, and Enthusiasm.

Along with a very comprehensive interpretation of the college's mission, the college needs to have a broad vision. Again, this vision needs to be articulated by the college president. According to Vaughan (1989), if community colleges are to achieve their full potential, then the president must communicate the vision of the college. For example, if a group of physicians proposes a continuing education class, the president should not reject it, stating that it is not within the purview of the college's mission. The president needs to get involved with a medical school and—through whatever means, including the use of technological advances—to provide whatever continuing education may be needed. Awareness that the community college is the only game in town for rural constituencies is critical and extremely important to the community college's ability to live up to its potential.

The secret to providing comprehensive services is through strategic planning, community education, collaborating with other agencies, and building coalitions. With the savings realized from the sharing of resources, the community and the college can focus on the nontraditional populations and provide comprehensive services. These services need to go well beyond the traditional university parallel and technical education areas. These services need to move into community service, cultural affairs, economic development, in-plant training, literacy, and collaborative programs with local school divisions.

The Rural Community College as a Catalyst

The comprehensive mission of the rural community college places it in a critical leadership role within its service area communities. The community college should be the catalyst that pulls the total community together in a very positive, focused direction. In a 1992 issue of the *Community College Review,* Mawby cited the critical role the community college must play in the decades to come. He views the major role of the community college as being one of a catalyst and a collaborator. He observes that the majority of our elected officials do not have the vision, commitment, and concern for the "whole" and instead focus on a limited constituency. At the same time, he notes, localities are being asked more and more to provide services for the community that federal and state governments had previously been providing. Since the problems of society are complex, the solutions must be comprehensive and involve collaboration, and problem solvers have to deal with the general resistance to change, and the persistence of "turfism" in addressing societal needs.

Mawby's observations are certainly true of the service area of rural community colleges. Rural community colleges must be willing to accept the challenge of providing the leadership that will pull the community together. The community college needs to coordinate the efforts of public education, social services, four-year colleges, and the business community. It needs to be the vehicle that opens up the lines of communication. The community college should provide the neutrality that encourages and nourishes the collaboration of the total community to ensure that there is a pooling of resources in order to benefit the total constituency. The rural community college needs to be the catalyst that drives community pride and togetherness. It needs to be at the heart of the total community.

Environmental Scanning and Strategic Planning

The rural community college must be heavily involved in environmental scanning and strategic planning. Several reports (Hauptman, 1991; El-Khawas, 1991) have outlined the challenges facing higher education in the future, including voter disinclination toward tax increases, which affects those community colleges that depend significantly on local revenues.

The challenges facing the nation at large have an even greater impact on rural community colleges. Anne McNutt (1994) pointed out that because rural areas are diverse, ranging from wealthy to impoverished communities, tax bases vary significantly. A lack of industry in many rural areas also translates into a lack of an adequate tax base. Unfortunately, in rural areas, it is the educational system that suffers first and foremost.

Rural community colleges are forced to anticipate community needs, funding sources, and local and state financial shortfalls. This can only be accomplished through a comprehensive planning process that includes environmental scanning—a process that focuses on identifying, studying, and analyzing current and emerging issues and forces that influence people in their service areas (Boone, 1992). Through continual environmental scanning, the colleges will not only be able to stay abreast of changes within their service areas, but also be able to have a greater understanding of how these forces affect the quality of life and the needs of the people within the community.

Continual environmental scanning coupled with the development of comprehensive strategic plans will enable the rural community college to be proactive rather than reactive in providing quality services to the people within the community and will ensure that the college maintains its comprehensive mission.

Educational Politics

If a rural community college is going to be successful in meeting the educational needs of its community, the college will have to be an expert in the politics of education. It is the responsibility of the college to let the community and the political jurisdictions know about its mission and accomplishments. Boone (1992) discussed the importance of community-based programming to community colleges and pointed out that although community leaders may not always be directly involved in the college's current efforts to resolve issues that have negative impacts on the quality of life of the people within the service area, they may very well be involved in future efforts. It is only by being aware of what the college is doing and the results of these efforts that the community will truly understand the mission of the college and the impact that it has on the service area. This awareness will in the end lead the community to support the college. For example, county administrators will need to be committed to the college's mission and will need to understand that community colleges will drive the economic development initiatives within the community.

The president is the political educator of the institution and has the responsibility for making state legislators aware of the college's mission and helping them understand the mission in order to ensure their support and commitment to providing resources for the college. It is the responsibility of the president to bring together, in a nonthreatening way, all the power of the political community to support the mission of the community college for the betterment of the total community. This is true of all community colleges but especially for rural community colleges. It is through pulling together the total forces of the community that rural community colleges will be able to address successfully the concern regarding funding inequities between rural and urban community colleges.

Economic Development

Economic development and community services provide outreach to our rural constituents. Practically everything we do is economic development and will help to improve our communities. University parallel curricula, technical education, continuing education, in-plant training, literacy programs, and community impact studies; all of these encourage business and industry to locate in a region. Cultural experiences, art, and music are also very important parts of community (economic) development. All of these are essential if our communities are to grow. It is only through the leadership of the rural community college that our communities will develop the holistic approaches to broad-based education which would include K-12 education as well as both formal and informal adult education provided by community colleges.

Quality Instruction

Whether rural or urban, community colleges need to recognize that the hallmark of their service is being "student friendly" and providing quality instruction. The "rubber meets the road" in the classroom and the classroom extends well beyond the developed college campus. The campus may be a storefront or a room in a library or in a prison. It is wherever a significant number of students come together that the college provides instruction, and it must be quality instruction.

With new technology for distance learning, and much more sophisticated equipment to provide expanded interactive audiovisual format, community colleges need to look at ways of going even further to provide educational opportunities to a wide range of students. With distance learning technology, community colleges will not only be able to provide training for traditional students, but will also be able to provide opportunities for those needing baccalaureate programs, graduate programs, and continuing education for professionals such as dentists, doctors, lawyers, and engineers. Distance learning opens up a whole new vista for collaborative efforts with other educational providers.

A word of caution: We educators have a tendency to look for panaceas. Distance learning is not a substitute for what exciting and innovative faculty members can offer. As we embark on this new dimension, community colleges need to go slowly. Through staff development for faculty and through careful research into distance learning programs, colleges will allay fears and will come closer to the user friendly instruction that has become our hallmark.

Future Challenges for Rural Community Colleges

Marketing the Community College Product. Community colleges, on both a national level and a local level, have done a very poor job of getting the message out to the people, to local entities, and to state and nationally elected representatives. Community colleges have been the most innovative entity in education in the twentieth century. Unfortunately, the general community and political leaders do not fully comprehend the mission, the variety of services provided, and the tremendous successes of the community college. Community college leaders have no one to blame but themselves. We have done a poor job in marketing our product. We need to get much better at articulating our mission, our accomplishments, and our plans.

A critical issue in marketing our product is why we do not buy it ourselves. If we are so good and so essential to the development of our community, then why are we so reluctant to buy our product. If the CEO of an automobile company does not drive its brand vehicle, the board of directors of that company would probably not continue the employment of the CEO. How many community college presidents buy their own product? That is, how many community college presidents' children are graduates of their colleges?

How can we go out to our community and tell them how good we are when we do not send our children to our own community colleges? Buying what we sell has to start at the top and should be the keystone of any community college marketing plan. We can certainly gain a great deal of credibility within the service region if members of our family are attending our community college. I know for a fact that the quality of education at most community colleges is at least as good as that of flagship universities within their area, and I buy our college's product.

Ensuring a People-Friendly Environment. People who have not experienced higher education before, who are the first generation of their families to attend college, and who come from rural settings, represent a fragile constituency. They often question their ability to be successful and they tend to suffer from low self-esteem. These individuals frequently come from environments in which they have not been encouraged or stimulated to learn and to develop their potential. Rural colleges in particular need to provide an environment where people feel comfortable, without regard to their backgrounds or goals. Faculty, staff, and administrators need to be extremely sensitive to this group of students, and go out of their way if necessary to make the college experience a welcoming one. The total college family is responsible for ensuring that the college's reputation is one of making people feel comfortable at the college and with the services that the college provides.

The most important area in which rural community colleges must assure a "people friendly" environment is in the area of financial aid. In many rural colleges, it is not uncommon for 80 percent or more of the students to be eligible for some form of financial aid. It is essential that a mechanism be developed to support these individuals in their initial experience (which is usually applying for financial aid) and as they become involved with higher education.

Continuing to Promote Egalitarianism. At the heart of the mission of "democracy's colleges" is egalitarianism. No institution in our society cuts across race, class, age, and gender lines like the community college. The community college represents a human mosaic. We educate more women than any other type of higher education institution, we educate more minorities, and we educate more older people. Our constituents mirror our communities. Besides providing a formal educational experience, community colleges bring groups together in a congenial, nonthreatening setting where community goals can be developed and embraced. Without a doubt, the accomplishment that community colleges can be most proud of is that they have opened up educational opportunities to a broader group of people, and are working toward breaking down barriers formerly imposed by race, class, gender, and age divisions. The future challenge to rural community colleges will be to remember this and continue to open up educational opportunities.

A Challenge for Higher Education

Community colleges may have to take on another important challenge: the restructuring of higher education. Higher education in the United States has been successful since the establishment of Harvard College in the seventeenth century. Times have changed, and needs have changed as well, but higher education has remained unchanged in most respects. Community colleges, as the newcomers to the system, need to continue a visionary role and look for innovative ways to reorganize higher education.

Resources for higher education are dwindling and the nation's love affair with higher education is coming under question. Providing a country club setting for recent high school graduates no longer serves our young people well and is something we can no longer afford. We need to become risk-takers and, through introspection, revisit the mission of higher education and question if the traditional methods of delivery are still the best methods. Do we need more campuses or can we use community facilities? Should we have four-year colleges offering the same first two years of college that community colleges are already providing most effectively? Or should we embrace the concept of upper-division and lower-division colleges? Should we consider changing the paradigm by enhancing research and professional schools rather than duplicating the first two years of college?

Higher education must look at collaboration and cooperation and move away from duplication of effort. Since higher education is the organization that educates society's leaders, we need to be prepared to lead the way toward rebuilding our own house to the point where we are more responsive to the needs of our communities.

References

Bogart, Q. J. "The Community College Mission." In G. A. Baker (ed.), *A Handbook on the Community College in America: Its History, Mission, and Management.* Westport, Conn.: Greenwood Press, 1994.

Boone, E. J. "Community-Based Programming: An Opportunity and Imperative for the Community College." *Community College Review,* 1992, *20* (3), 8–20.

El-Khawas, E. *Campus Trends, 1991.* Higher Education Panel Report no. 81. Washington, D.C.: American Council on Education, 1991.

Harlacher, E. L., and Gollattscheck, J. F. "Building Learning Communities." *Community College Review,* 1992, *20* (3), 29–36.

Hauptman, A. M. "Meeting the Challenge: Doing More with Less in the 1990s." *Educational Record,* 1991, *72* (2), 6–13.

McNutt, A. S. "Rural Community Colleges: Meeting the Challenges of the 1990s." In G. A. Baker (ed.), *A Handbook on the Community College in America: Its History, Mission, and Management.* Westport, Conn.: Greenwood Press, 1994.

Mawby, R. G. "The Role of the Community College in the Decade of Community." *Community College Review,* 1992, *20* (3), 21–25.

Roueche, J. E., Baker, G. A., and Rose, R. R. *Shared Vision: Transformational Leadership in American Community Colleges.* Washington, D.C.: Community College Press, American Association of Community and Junior Colleges, National Center for Higher Education, 1989.

Vaughan, G. B. *Leadership in Transition: The Community College Presidency.* New York: American Council on Education/Macmillan, 1989.

JOHN CAVAN is president of Southside Virginia Community College, Alberta.

*In this case example of a rural community college, the president traces
the college's recent efforts to reposition itself in order to increase its
effectiveness as a viable community organization.*

The Small Rural Community College in 1994 and Beyond: One President's View

Donald L. Reichard

Small rural community colleges are at a crossroads, as are the communities
they serve. Rural institutions such as government, schools, families, and businesses are stressed as they face the emerging global society (Treadway, 1992).
The problems facing the rural United States in the mid 1990s are many:
poverty, illiteracy, a graying population, dying small towns, a shortage of
trained workers, substandard housing, high unemployment, above-average
school dropout rates, substance abuse, and the lack of adequate health care
and child care (Vineyard, 1993; Commission on Small/Rural Community Colleges, 1992). Although most of these problems exist in urban areas, they are
often more serious and more difficult to address in rural areas.

Today, like the communities they serve, small rural community colleges
and their presidents find themselves confronted by a host of critical issues.
Many of the problems are not new. In the seventies, much attention was
focused on the particular problems of small rural two-year colleges: inadequate
funding and staffing, maintaining curriculum breadth, providing access, student recruitment and retention, the need for increased marketing, and faculty
recruitment (Vineyard, 1979). Many of these same problems remain unre-
solved (Wiess and others, 1986–1987; Institute of Policy Sciences and Public
Affairs, 1989; Vineyard, 1993; Prager, 1993; Commission on Small/Rural Community Colleges, 1992). And new challenges have arisen: institutional effectiveness and accountability, the need for program-specific accreditation, the
sweep of new educational technology and its high cost, greater need for faculty and staff development, the need to revitalize existing curricula, urgent
demands to start new programs, and governance questions on regionalism and
centralization.

Confronted by such societal and institutional problems, small rural community colleges have had to assess the effectiveness of their operations and reexamine their role in the communities they serve. Looking back over the last several years at the changes made at James Sprunt Community College (JSCC), and looking ahead to the year 2000, a number of key issues and questions about how best to respond emerge. The first is funding. How will small rural community colleges be able to do more with less when they are already severely underfunded? The second is planning. Can the adoption of strategic planning and more focused operational planning improve institutional effectiveness? The third is leadership and organization. Can the implementation of team-management and transformational leadership practices increase productivity and results? The fourth is the role of a community college as a community change agent. How can a community college expand its mission in community development to improve the quality of life for the rural citizens it serves?

The recent experiences at James Sprunt Community College (JSCC) serve as a case study for this chapter. The college is small and rural as witnessed by the following background information. JSCC is located in southeastern North Carolina, and serves rural Duplin County (population 40,000). There are ten small towns in the county, the largest having a population of 3,000. Most of the county's 819 square miles are devoted to farming and poultry and livestock operations, primarily the swine industry. The major employer is the textile industry with three major yarn plants and numerous apparel companies. James Sprunt enrolls 1,000 credit and 2,300 noncredit students each quarter. The average age of the students is twenty-nine. More than 65 percent of the students are female, 60 percent attend full-time and the vast majority work full- or part-time. James Sprunt, like other community colleges in North Carolina, offers comprehensive services including college-transfer, occupational, continuing education, literacy, and community service programs.

Funding

It is difficult to believe that by 1994 more has not been done to address the underfunding of small rural community colleges. In 1976, the Task Force on Rural Community Colleges stated, "Any system of division of resources among institutions which is based upon equal funding per unit is an inequitable system and is prejudicial against the smaller rural community college" (Vineyard, 1979, p. 37). By 1986, Sullins and Atwell reported that "there does exist some recognition of the additional costs associated with operating small colleges" (1986, p. 47). Even where some differential funding was being provided, it could not be shown that it was enough to equalize funding. Vineyard (1993) recently revisited the situation and did not report any progress.

North Carolina. In 1989, North Carolina recognized the need to distribute state funds on a more equitable basis among its fifty-eight community colleges (Commission on the Future of the North Carolina Community College System, 1989). In addition, the funding formula problem was being magnified by severe underfunding. The per-student expenditure had fallen to 25 percent or more below the national median (Commission on the Future of the North Carolina Community College System, 1989, p. 13). For small colleges like James Sprunt, the deficit was even higher because of the inequities in the funding formula. In response, the state legislature committed itself to restoring adequate funding. However, the goal of $135 million new dollars ran up against lean economic times. Thus, five years later, only a net of $13 million new dollars have been appropriated to the system. The new funding formula has never been implemented.

James Sprunt. Since 1989, the college's small portion of the $13 million, plus other funds stemming from enrollment growth, have had to be used to increase faculty and staff salaries and to maintain services. Meanwhile, fixed costs have continued to rise. New positions in institutional research, institutional effectiveness, computer operations, counseling, and instructional support have been mandated without additional funding. Therefore, the system and its colleges are more underfunded today than five years ago.

The response to this worsening fiscal picture has been twofold. First, the system has cut funding for selected programs and second, its colleges have attempted to do more with less through changes to internal operations. Funds for the system's Visiting Artist and community-service programs have all but been eliminated. The former program funded a visiting artist for each college to provide artistic and cultural education for youth and adults. The latter program enabled a wide range of vocational, avocational, and academic enrichment courses to be offered throughout the college's service area. It has become obvious that rural citizens are being hurt much more than their urban counterparts by the cutback in funding to these programs. Larger institutions have been able to keep the programs going by replacing state funds with local resources. Also, urban citizens have been able to obtain cultural programming and self-improvement courses from other sources, which are not available in rural areas. Thus, the small rural community colleges and their populations are the ones being deprived.

Further funding disadvantages exist for small rural colleges because of the sparse populations they serve. This results in smaller classes that generate fewer dollars, even though smaller institutions offer many of the same programs at close to the same cost as larger institutions (Institute of Policy Sciences and Public Affairs, 1989). Likewise, it is more difficult for rural colleges to raise external funds either through grants (because they lack the staff to prepare proposals) or through their foundations (because their service areas are typically poorer).

Future. The report by the Institute of Policy Sciences and Public Affairs at Duke University succinctly states that "spending a lot more money on rural community colleges would certainly solve most of their difficulties" (1989, p. 1). Another new funding formula is now being designed. Legislative strategies continue to be deployed in an effort to increase funding. Further delay in acquiring increased funding will only widen the gap in the ability of small colleges to provide equitable educational opportunities to their rural citizens.

Consequently, the small rural community colleges in North Carolina may have to band together in a formal manner not unlike what was done nationally with the earlier formation of the Commission on Small/Rural Community Colleges. The presidents of small rural community colleges need to become much more politically active and astute. Another opportunity to increase both the legislature's awareness of and willingness to resolve the funding problem can come by increasing colleges' local alliances with business and industry and other powerful political players. It is James Sprunt's goal to do this in part by implementing a new community-based programming process, which is discussed below. The second response to continued underfunding has been an attempt by colleges to do more with less. Efforts at James Sprunt have focused on its planning, leadership, organizational, and management practices.

Planning

An effective planning process including budget planning is essential for a small rural college hampered by severe fiscal constraints. Two examples will serve to illustrate the importance. First, one of the planning assumptions made for James Sprunt's long-range plan (1988–1993) was that very little enrollment increase would occur. However, over the next five-year period the college's enrollment increased greatly. Second, during the mid eighties, low enrollment in the college's two associate degree programs in poultry and livestock and agribusiness prompted the decision to close these programs. However, a large protest was made by the agricultural community. Subsequently, the college postponed closure pending the outcome of a needs assessment among its agricultural and agribusiness industries. The results confirmed that the scene of agriculture had changed but the college had not changed with it. Swine production was quickly becoming a major new livestock industry in Duplin and surrounding counties, creating a need for many swine farm managers. Both of these examples demonstrate that the college's planning practices were failing to reveal windows of opportunity. Particularly lacking was a continuous practice of environmental scanning (Friedel and Rosenberg, 1993). The process also lacked a strategic emphasis. It was focused on operational planning based on past experience (Cope, 1987).

Revamped Planning. Based on the belief that if the college was going to progress it had to become more proactive in determining its future, a revamping of the college's planning processes was begun in 1988–1989. Using the College Council (a collegewide representational group) as the planning group, the following steps were taken:

1. The College Council schooled itself on strategic planning (Cope, 1987) and revisited its operational planning process.
2. The president appointed himself as the college's chief planning officer.

3. The planning group led the college in the development of a shared vision for the future.
4. The mission statement was rewritten with greater clarity.
5. Planning was simplified by developing new institutional goals upon which all subsequent operational plans would be based.
6. Institutional objectives were developed for each goal based on collegewide functional areas rather than by division or department, which enhanced team-management.
7. An assessment plan for each goal was created and the use of the results tied to subsequent planning cycles.
8. Scanning practices were increased, including the development of an institutional factbook.
9. The college began to use strategic planning. For the first time, several major areas of strategic emphasis were identified.
10. Planning became broad-based. For example, institutional objectives were built from both top-down and bottom-up processes, which came together at the College Council. Also, each employee's professional development plan had to be tied in part to the accomplishment of institutional objectives and goals.
11. Budget planning was incorporated into the strategic planning cycle. The planning and budgeting calendars were merged. Budget requests had to include justification based on institutional objectives and goals.

Strategic Planning. Returning to the need for strategic planning, the College Council initially identified four areas of strategic emphasis for the 1988–1993 long-range plan. These were expanding programs and services to business and industry, enhancing students' achievement of identified educational and career goals, increasing the college's efforts to reduce the rate of illiteracy, and achieving financial stability. To give closer operational attention to the implementation of these strategic initiatives, ad hoc teams were created for the business and industry and literacy areas. The student success initiative was assigned to the student services committee, while the financial stability issue was assigned to the president and his senior staff group. The ad hoc groups had representatives from all departments related to their strategic areas. Each group went through a period of research and education to better understand its own strategic initiative and each other's efforts and to identify windows of opportunity through which to proceed. To help identify new strategies, comparisons were made with peer institutions who appeared to be doing a better job (benchmarking) (Chaffee and Sherr, 1992). Periodic meetings focused on progress being made in implementing institutional objectives, sharing information, and modifying strategies as needed.

In 1991, during the college's biannual review of its mission and goals, two new strategic areas were added: incorporating an international focus across the curriculum (Greenfield, 1990) and implementing a community-based programming model. As with earlier strategic initiatives, an ad hoc group was created to oversee the internationalization initiative. For community-based programming, a team of trustees, community leaders, administrators, and faculty was constituted to begin learning the components of the community-based programming process.

Leadership and Organization

The changes in planning made at James Sprunt were based on team-management and transformational leadership principles (Roueche, Baker, and Rose, 1989; Roueche and Baker, 1987) and accompanied by reorganization of the college's decision-making structures and processes. The goals of reorganization were to improve the college's climate, morale, and communications; to reallocate resources from administrative to instructional purposes; and to establish an overall sense of common purpose. It was believed that by involving and empowering the faculty and staff, better decisions would result—thus enhancing the institution's effectiveness. A description of the major steps taken and the changes made follows.

Philosophy. A clear educational philosophy was established and articulated by the president. Central to this philosophy were several fundamental tenets. First, the college believed that educating students was foremost and that students were the center of the college. Faculty, counselors, and program heads were assigned equal responsibility and made the preeminent designers of a total student development program. The purpose of administrative and other personnel was to lead, facilitate, and support the educational enterprise as appropriate. A final tenet was that all employees were equal members of a collegewide team. And each was very much responsible for the success of students or clients and the college as a whole. To clearly demonstrate this egalitarian approach, all reserved parking on campus was abolished.

Reorganization. The administrative structure was streamlined and flattened, and the number of senior staff was reduced. Anthony's (1989) description of the context of the flat-matrix organization fits James Sprunt well. The funds saved through reorganization were reallocated to support the college's instructional programs. Structurally, all educational and student development programs were placed under one senior administrator. This organizational approach promoted collaboration among faculty and student services personnel and enhanced the integration necessary to establish a comprehensive student development program. This also enabled the president to give attention to other matters by reducing the time devoted to conflict management among several senior educational officers. Another change was to move department heads from administrative to instructional positions and have them carry some teaching responsibilities. The college also conducted an efficiency and staffing study to identify ways to save on the costs of operation.

The Team as Hero. A team-oriented management approach was implemented by revising decision-making and communication strategies (Hammons, 1992). The purpose, makeup, and operation of standing committees were revised. Faculty would predominate on committees. Senior administrators were charged with direct management responsibility to see that committees operated. Guidelines were produced on how to hold effective meetings. The role of the College Council as the key planning team for the institution was reemphasized. It was made clear that any issue could be brought forth by any individual or group for discussion at the monthly meetings of the council without fear of repercussions. Also, as described earlier, ad hoc teams were established as needed to plan and monitor the college's progress among its strategic areas of emphasis.

The Board of Trustees also commenced using its committee structure. Its committees began to meet prior to regular sessions with appropriate senior administrators and staff to discuss the college's efforts. This enhanced the trustees' understanding of college operations and also gave them the opportunity to provide their suggestions and ideas.

To promote fuller and more open communication, much emphasis was placed on information sharing. The president instituted quarterly meetings with the chairpersons of the college's five internal groups of employees, and periodic meetings with the faculty. A Student Advisory Council was created and began meeting quarterly. The president agreed to respond in writing at subsequent meetings to concerns raised by students. Finally, greater use of the college's weekly news bulletin by all groups to communicate their activities was encouraged. It was made clear that all institutional information, except that protected by privacy statutes, was available. This included such data as the salaries of all employees.

The examples cited above reflect an interlocking team style of operation. As Acebo (1989) points out, this model makes the team (whether it is a subgroup or the whole college) the hero—the central figure—rather than assigning that role to one or several of its members. In this model, "where all staff are responsible for the well-being of the entire institution, the therapeutic leader is responsible for the well-being of all staff" (Anthony, 1989, p. 1).

Morale. Practices to promote the well-being and morale of faculty, students, and staff were adopted. Examples included starting a wellness program, designing a new personnel classification and salary plan, upgrading salaries, instituting Fridays as a casual-dress day and a no-tie dress code during warm months, working a four-day week during summer quarter, refocusing the annual spring fling event on staff and student competitions and camaraderie, and starting a faculty and staff appreciation day with the activities designed by a new group each year. The appearance of the campus was not overlooked. A landscaping and maintenance plan was designed and implemented to make the buildings and grounds more attractive. Symbolic of this effort, a campus cleanup day was held wherein the custodial staff served as the leaders for groups of faculty and staff. The role reversal was a real morale booster. With the exception of the salary plan, all the above practices were implemented at very little cost.

Results

Despite tight budgets, and although success has not been equal in all strategic areas, progress has been made. For example, literacy enrollment has increased by over 30 percent (Office of Institutional Research, 1993). Programs and services for business and industry have increased—as has their support for the college, especially through increased giving to the college's foundation. Budget stability now allows the institution to begin each year with a reserve. For students, retention and completion rates have increased somewhat, and enrollment in curriculum and occupational extension programs has increased greatly. Overall, even though service area population decreased from 1980 to 1990, the percentage served by the college increased from 11 percent in 1986 to 19 percent in 1993 (Office of Institutional Research, 1993).

Qualitatively, with the leadership of the dean of academic and student services, the total student development program has been enhanced. Refinements have been made to the competency-based format for courses and programs. A new academic advising system and a faculty mentoring program have been implemented. Initial steps have been taken to implement a student tracking system. Tutoring services have been expanded and services have been added for the disabled. Transportation service was started for students taking English as a Second Language (ESL) classes. Funds to support child care have been increased. And, most recently, a new student leadership training program has been launched. In keeping with the emphasis on planning and assessment, program evaluation has received much closer attention. Unproductive programs have been stopped while new programs have been started in response to the changing workforce needs of the area. Besides swine management, programs have been developed in allied health and in quality improvement for the textile industry. Also, the capacity of programs has been better planned. For example, with the shortage of nurses abating, the college will reduce the size of its nursing program two years from now; therefore, the most recent faculty member was hired for only a two-year period.

Most encouraging about the leadership, organizational, planning, and budgeting practices that have been installed is that they seem to be working! The literature on leadership continues to emphasize the need for organizational structures and leadership behaviors that promote empowerment, collaboration, and coalition building (Baker, 1992; Birnbaum, 1992; Duncan and Harlacher, 1990; Fryer and Lovas, 1991). For small rural community colleges, there is also a real need to extend such practices into their communities. That is why James Sprunt so quickly embraced its latest strategic area of emphasis in community-based programming.

Community-Based Programming

The need and potential for rural community colleges to serve as a leading agent for community change is not new. In 1979, Vineyard spoke on behalf of the

Task Force on Rural Community Colleges: "The community college represents an ideal catalyst for addressing many of the problems of rural life" (p. 34). However, given the current problems facing our rural communities, it appears that most of our small rural community colleges have not been able to fill the role of catalyst for community development to the extent needed. That is not to say that outreach efforts have not been attempted or successful (for example, see Barry and Carter, 1989; Weiss, 1985). But, in most cases, collaboration has been with other service and educational agencies most closely aligned with the college's mission in workforce training, transfer education, and so forth. Such efforts have helped community colleges to expand their missions and to grow but have not been necessarily helpful in solving the pressing social, economic, or educational issues facing their communities (Gillett-Karam and Killacky, 1994).

Recently, there has been a renewed call for community colleges to emphasize community needs and community collaboration in their efforts. The American Association of Community Colleges' Building Communities Program and the League for Innovation's Catalysts for Community Change program (LeCroy, 1993) are examples. Why is there this urgent call for community colleges, urban and rural, to take bold action? As we approach the twenty-first century, the problems facing our nation's communities are unprecedented and need immediate attention (Crawford, 1989). As Crawford so clearly states: "They [community colleges] have no choice but to become involved in the fundamental issues facing their communities and the nation—the fates of both hang in the balance" (1989, p. 2). This is particularly true for our rural community colleges and their communities.

But there is a different and much greater risk in the kind of community leadership Crawford speaks about than the sort of collaboration with community agencies and leaders conducted previously. Sensitive political issues can emerge, turfism can rear up, and community leaders may well question whether such a catalyst role is valid for the community college. Another major block preventing more involvement is the lack of skills among administrators, faculty, and staff to effectively implement this newer role. Community colleges have also lacked a systematic approach by which to guide their efforts into these more-or-less uncharted and risky waters.

The Academy for Community College Leadership Advancement, Innovation and Modeling—Project ACCLAIM. James Sprunt's involvement with Project ACCLAIM at North Carolina State University is an attempt to gain the requisite skills needed to move into these unexplored areas. ACCLAIM and its community-based programming model challenge the community college to reexamine its community emphasis, conduct environmental scanning, identify major issues and serve as a leader or catalyst in creating coalitions to address and resolve these issues (Boone, 1992; Gillett-Karam and Killacky, 1994; Killacky, 1994; Moore and Feldt, 1993; Crawford, 1989).

Institutionalization. During 1992–1993, the president and a team consisting of sixteen trustees, community leaders, faculty, and staff completed a community-based programming (C-BP) training institute. The team was exposed to and engaged in learning tasks focused on the fifteen process tasks within the model. The first team has moved ahead with field-testing the C-BP model. The college has chosen to field-test the C-BP model with the issue of illiteracy. The high rate of illiteracy was ranked as one of the most serious issues facing the county. A literacy subcommittee will guide the college's efforts as it attempts to implement the tasks called for in the model (Boone, 1992). During 1993–1994, a second team of twenty college and community leaders was trained and will apply the model to another major issue in the service area.

Although only in the second year of the project, several benefits have been seen already. The model has lent guidance to progress in another strategic area: service to business and industry and workforce preparedness. Such steps as tours of area industries by trustees and the College Council, attendance at various area Chamber of Commerce meetings, starting an annual business and industry appreciation breakfast, and obtaining membership for the president at a country club at the far end of the service area in order for the college to be more visible in that community are examples. In addition, principles from the C-BP model are being used by the county's economic development commission, with the college's assistance, to create a long-range strategic plan for economic development. Because of our recent outreach efforts through Project ACCLAIM, it is expected that the county commissioners will fund a new grants-writer position for the college to assist the county, community agencies, and the college in seeking external funding. Finally, because of its expanded role in the community, the time may be right for the college to launch a capital campaign to raise funds to build a multipurpose center on campus for use by the entire county and region.

Institutionalization of the C-BP model or other such mission-altering concepts, such as total quality management, is not an easy task (Chaffee and Sherr, 1992). This is very true for a small college with limited staff and resources. For example, freeing mid-level literacy staff and faculty from their primary duties so they can practice and learn C-BP skills is costly and time consuming. However, if lasting change is to be effective, this must occur.

Through community-based programming, it is the college's goal to help empower its rural constituents. Hopefully, rural citizens and groups using the college as a resource and catalyst will be able to on their own "access, process, and use information to solve their own local problems" (Galbraith, 1992, p. 145). The college's experience thus far has been very encouraging. As Galbraith asserts, "Institutions which are accepting responsibility to become partners with rural communities, industry, and government are finding a high level of receptivity and involvement toward needed reforms" (1992, p. 148).

Conclusion

With the many demands facing the presidents of small rural community colleges, role conflicts have emerged. Many of the forces shaping the future of our institutions are requiring presidents to devote much time to external matters. Presidents need to work simultaneously at expanding the college's community and economic development roles, increasing resources and revising funding formulas through political action at the local, state, and national levels, raising external funds through foundation activities, improving articulation with the public schools and four-year colleges, and improving strategic planning practices.

However, many faculty and staff within our small rural institutions are reluctant to recognize any need for change in the role of their president. The highly visible and always-available president is still desired. And, indeed, where presidents of small colleges are carrying primary operational responsibility for certain functions due to lack of staff, refocusing efforts externally is extremely difficult. Keeping the "presidential seesaw," as Vaughan (1986) calls it, in balance has become an extremely delicate task. Or, as Vaughan (1994) describes more recently, choosing in which areas to exercise presidential leadership has become a key question.

The adoption of situational leadership and team-management practices to empower the faculty, staff, and students can help small rural community colleges progress while also enabling their presidents to give greater attention to external opportunities. The success of our small rural community colleges may be increased by joining forces with our rural constituencies. In order to do so, the role of the presidents to provide leadership in and devote time to the external environment will have to be accepted and supported (Duncan and Harlacker, 1990). It is this role of the president that the future demands. As recently stated by the head of a large corporation, "A CEO has two main jobs: to live in the future and to pick good people. If I don't live in the future, the enterprise won't have a future" (Brown, 1994, p. 19).

References

Acebo, S. "The Team as Hero: A Paradigm Shift in College Leadership." *Leadership Abstracts,* 1992, 5 (4), 1–2.

Anthony, J. H. "Therapeutic Leadership." *Leadership Abstracts,* 1989, 2 (13), 1–2.

Baker, G. A., and Associates. *Cultural Leadership.* Washington, D.C.: Community College Press, 1992.

Barry, P. O., and Carter, K. G. "Partnerships: Survival Techniques for a Small College." *Small College Creativity,* 1989, 1 (1), 4–9.

Birnbaum, R. *How Academic Leadership Works: Understanding Success and Failure in the College Presidency.* San Francisco: Jossey-Bass, 1992.

Boone, E. J. "Community-Based Programming: An Opportunity and Imperative for the Community College." *Community College Review,* 1992, 20 (3), 8–20.

Brown, T. "Looking Back Can Help Others See Ahead." *Industry Week,* 1994, 243 (4), 19.

Chaffee, E. E., and Sherr, L. A. *Quality: Transforming Postsecondary Education.* ASHE-ERIC Higher Education Report No. 3. Washington, D.C.: School of Education and Human Development, George Washington University, 1992.

Commission on Small/Rural Community Colleges. *Forgotten Minorities: Rural Americans and the Colleges That Serve Them.* Washington, D.C.: American Association of Community Colleges, 1992. (ED 351 054)

Commission on the Future of the North Carolina Community College System. *Gaining the Competitive Edge: The Challenge to North Carolina's Community Colleges.* Durham, N.C.: MDC, 1989. (ED 303 302)

Cope, R. G. *Opportunity from Strength: Strategic Planning Clarified with Case Examples.* ASHE-ERIC Higher Education Report No. 8. Washington, D.C.: Association for the Study of Higher Education, 1987.

Crawford, M. E. "No Choice but to Be Involved." *Leadership Abstracts,* 1989, 2 (21), 1–2.

Duncan, A. H., and Harlacker, E. L. "The Twenty-first Century Executive Leadership." *Community College Review,* 1990, *18* (4), 39–47.

Friedel, J. N., and Rosenberg, D. "Environmental Scanning Practices in Junior, Technical, and Community Colleges." *Community College Review,* 1993, *20* (5), 16–22.

Fryer, T. W., Jr., and Lovas, J. C. *Leadership in Governance: Creating Conditions for Successful Decision Making in the Community College.* San Francisco: Jossey-Bass, 1991.

Galbraith, M. W. (ed.). *Education in the Rural American Community: A Lifelong Process.* Malabar, Fla.: Krieger, 1992.

Gillett-Karam, R., and Killacky, J. "Pathways to Tomorrow: A Conversation About Community-Based Programming." *Journal of the Community Development Society,* 1994, *25* (1), 111–122.

Greenfield, R. K. (ed.). *Developing International Education Programs.* New Directions for Community Colleges, no. 70. San Francisco: Jossey-Bass, 1990.

Hammons, J. O. "To Acquire Stature: To Thine Own Self Be True." In B. W. Dziech and W. R. Vilter (eds.), *Prisoners of Elitism: The Community College's Struggle for Stature.* New Directions for Community Colleges, no. 78. San Francisco: Jossey-Bass, 1992.

Institute of Policy Sciences and Public Affairs. *Rural Community Colleges in North Carolina.* Durham, N.C.: Duke University, 1989.

Killacky, J. "Colleges Learn Community-Based Programming." *Rural Adult Education Forum,* 1994, *6* (3), 6–7.

LeCroy, N. A. (ed.). *Catalysts for Community Change.* Mission Viejo, Calif.: League for Innovation in the Community College, 1993.

Moore, A. B., and Feldt, J. A. *Facilitating Community and Decision-Making Groups.* Malabar, Fla.: Krieger, 1993.

Office of Institutional Research. *JSCC Factbook.* Kenansville, N.C.: James Sprunt Community College, 1993.

Prager, C. (ed.). *Accreditation of the Two-Year College.* New Directions for Community Colleges, no. 83. San Francisco: Jossey-Bass, 1993.

Roueche, J. E., and Baker, G. A. *Access and Excellence.* Washington, D.C.: Community College Press, 1987.

Roueche, J. E., Baker, G. A., and Rose, R. R. *Shared Vision: Transformational Leadership in American Community Colleges.* Washington, D.C.: Community College Press, American Association of Community and Junior Colleges, National Center for Higher Education, 1989.

Sullins, W. R., and Atwell, C. A. "The Role of Small Rural Community Colleges in Providing Access." *Community College Review,* 1986, *13* (4), 45–51.

Treadway, D. M. "Higher Education." In M. W. Galbraith (ed.), *Education in the Rural American Community: A Lifelong Process.* Malabar, Fla.: Krieger, 1992.

Vaughan, G. B. "Balancing the Presidential Seesaw." *Southern Association of Community and Junior Colleges—Occasional Paper,* 1986, *4* (2), 1–3.

Vaughan, G. B. "Effective Presidential Leadership: Twelve Areas of Focus." In A. Cohen, F. Brawer, and Associates, *Managing Community Colleges: A Handbook for Effective Practice.* San Francisco: Jossey-Bass, 1994.

Vineyard, E. E. "American Association of Community and Junior Colleges Task Force Report: The Rural Community College." *Community College Review,* 1979, *6* (3), 29–45.

Vineyard, E. E. *The Pragmatic Presidency: Effective Leadership in the Two-Year College Setting.* Bolton, Mass.: Anker, 1993.

Weiss, M. "The Role of the Small/Rural Community Colleges Within Their Service Areas." Paper presented at the American Association of Community and Junior Colleges Convention, San Diego, Calif., Apr. 15, 1985. 7 pp. (ED 261 852)

Weiss, M., Bryden, B., Young, J., Sharples, D. K., Lidstrom, K., and Conrad, J. "What Are the Challenges Facing Small, Rural Community Colleges Today?" *Community, Technical, and Junior College Journal,* 1986–1987, 57 (3), 26–29.

DONALD L. REICHARD *is president of James Sprunt Community College in Kenansville, North Carolina.*

The place of tribal rural community colleges in U.S. higher education is examined, along with their history, their present scope and role, and their future.

Tribal Colleges: Their Role in U.S. Higher Education

Michael J. Hill

The tribal college movement officially began in 1968 with the founding of Navaho Community College at Many Farms, Arizona. As with any historical event, the preceding circumstances reveal much about the beliefs and motivations of the people involved. The beginning of that institution—the first tribal college and the others that followed it—can be more fully understood if history is explained. Moreover, the present situation of these highly specialized and esoteric institutions is drawn upon this background, as is the motivation of their leaders.

This chapter is presented in three parts. The first is a description of the historical context, which led to the belief on the part of Indians that their own postsecondary institutions were vitally necessary. The second is an examination of the present role and scope of the tribal colleges. And finally, the third section considers the future of these institutions.

Historical Context

A tribal college, by definition, is chartered by a tribal council representing a sovereign nation. Thus, the background of the tribal college movement is embedded partly in the history of the relations between nations—sometimes European nations, but chiefly between the United States and the five hundred or so nations now commonly called Indian tribes (Dobyns, 1983).

Europeans collectively named these many different peoples *Indians,* for essentially the same reason we refer to those people of the diverse countries of Japan, Korea, China, and so forth as Asians—as a categorical convenience. Although obviously too broad a classification, this misnomer is perhaps rep-

NEW DIRECTIONS FOR COMMUNITY COLLEGES, no. 90, Summer 1995 © Jossey-Bass Inc., Publishers

resentative of the misunderstandings Indians were to undergo in the next half millennium. However, for all its inaccuracy, it was and is a convenient catch-all term, and thus suits the purposes of this chapter. It should be recognized that many Indians continue to think of themselves as members of only one of the five hundred nations. Moreover, the worldview of Indians has frequently remained, to the present, largely local in orientation.

In terms of maintaining sovereignty and viability as a nation, Indians' original self-identification as members of separate, individual tribal groups was not the best stance to take, especially in view of the coming trials of disease, warfare, and forced relocation. One of the first struggles was the competition with the European colonists for land. For the European colonist, land was a prerequisite for suffrage, upward mobility, and economic security. For the Indian, land was communally controlled and religiously revered. Its control among Indians has been described as usership as opposed to ownership. Nevertheless, whatever the Indians felt for their homelands, it was not a match for the overwhelming numbers, greater organization, and cupidity of the colonists. Buttressing the colonists' motivation for land and its resources was the rationale that however poorer the Indians became they would be richer for access to the Christian religion and other aspects of European culture.

According to various colonial charters, schools to convert the heathen to civilized ways and Christianize them were to be established soon after the first beachheads. For example, with the founding of Harvard College and other Ivy League institutions came an accompanying mission to educate the Indians. The Indians did not reciprocate in this transaction. Most simply ignored these Christianizing and educative efforts as irrelevant to their needs or way of life (McLuhan, 1971). Those Indians who did attend schools and colleges found scant support or encouragement when they returned to their tribes. "Acquisition of such knowledge seemed to be confusing to young tribal members who observed conflicts between the ways of the white man and of their respective tribal communities" (McDonald, 1981, p. 20). From the very beginning, Indians believed the education of youth should remain within local control (Adams, 1974). However, as European inroads into the Americas increased, the Indians would soon not be allowed this privilege.

With federal support, the task of educating and Christianizing the Indians had begun by religious denominations very early in the colonial era and gained momentum during the latter part of the nineteenth century. By the 1880s, Indian nations were reaching the nadir of their power. This was the beginning of the Reservation Era, when almost all Indian nations were forced out of their historic homelands and onto much smaller land bases. By 1890, almost all Indians found drastic change for themselves and their children mandated by their new masters.

The first educational institutions to affect large numbers of Indians were government boarding schools, frequently operated by religious groups such as the Methodists or Catholics. One of the boarding schools' major boosters was Lieutenant Richard Henry Pratt. He felt that through intensive education and removal from the tribal culture he could remake the Indian into a white man. Pratt is quoted as saying, "In Indian civilization I am a Baptist, because I believe in immersing Indians in our civilization and . . . holding them there until they are thoroughly soaked" (Pratt, 1964, p. 335). Many other boarding schools followed, such as the Hampton Institute in Hampton, Virginia, the Carlisle Indian School in Carlisle, Pennsylvania, and the Haskell Indian School in Lawrence, Kansas (Tucker, 1979).

There was no involvement of Native American tribal groups in the planning or operation of these educational institutions. The main purpose of these schools was to separate Indians from their culture (Beck and Walters, 1977). The U.S. government and the church groups were vitally interested in the assimilation of the Indian into the mainstream culture. This was known as the vanishing policy. Indians were to disappear into the melting pot of the general population. Beside these assimilation efforts, Indians were fast disappearing anyway—in 1890, less than 250,000 could be counted. To document the vanishing race, a federal bureau was quickly created—the Bureau of American Ethnology—staffed by anthropologists carefully cataloging and storing on museum shelves what other white men had so recently tried to crush.

Indians have never forgotten that education was a primary tool in federal government and church group acculturation efforts. The focus of the efforts primarily was on the youth. "The classroom would be the place where the Indian would shed his 'savageness' and assume 'civilized' ways" (Fritz, 1963). The treasure of Indian languages would not be spared this process, either. In 1887, the Commissioner of Indian Affairs forbade the speaking of Indian languages in any reservation school (Annual Report of the Commissioner of Indian Affairs, 1987). Corporal punishment was given for speaking the language one had learned at home.

The early part of the twentieth century brought changes but was not any more of an encouraging time for Indian education than the preceding decades. Boarding schools such as Carlisle and Hampton Institute fell out of favor with Bureau of Indian Affairs (BIA) officials and Indians started attending boarding schools nearer to home, which were frequently located on their own reservation. Increasingly, they also attended day schools just like other U.S. students. As for colleges and universities, these were still primarily liberal arts institutions offering curricula that did not fit Indian needs (McDonald, 1981). Indian culture and language were completely ignored at all levels of education. BIA teachers courted dismissal if they incorporated in their teaching any of the rich and ancient heritage of the vast oral tradition. As a consequence entire generations of Indians grew up caught between two worlds in a kind of cultural limbo.

With the election of Franklin Roosevelt in 1932, there came hope that a new age was dawning. Roosevelt appointed John Collier as commissioner of the BIA in 1933. Collier saw Indian culture as a valuable heritage, which should be preserved. Due in large part to his efforts the Indian Reorganization Act (IRA) of 1934 was passed. The IRA enabled tribal groups to enhance their political and economic status at the local level. It recognized the strength of the communal landholding traditions by halting the assignment of tribal land to individuals. It also allowed tribes the option of formulating constitutions and incorporating with charters from the U.S. government, and it provided loans for postsecondary Native American education (Eder and Reyhner, 1989). By 1935, a trickle of 515 Indian students were attending colleges and universities under the provisions of the act (Tucker, 1979). But many leaders thought Collier to be too radical. They criticized his reforms. Religious leaders were horrified at a return to tribalism. Nevertheless, he held his post as commissioner and stayed the course until the end of World War II.

At the close of World War II, the influx of Indian veterans returning to the reservation with rights under the GI Bill stimulated a significant trend toward increased college attendance (Clark, 1972). During the ensuing years, many of these veterans became leaders in Indian affairs at the tribal and national level (McDonald, 1981). Some gained tribal council seats and were key supporters in the establishment of the first tribal colleges (Stein, 1988).

In the early 1960s, the BIA Higher Education Grant Program was created. In 1970, over 4,300 Native Americans received funds to attend college out of this program (Eschwage, 1971). The Higher Education Grant Program was successful in funding Indians interested in a college education, but their achievement was not high. A study of 2,000 Native American college students by the General Accounting Office in the 1970s found they had lower assessment test scores and lower grade point averages than the overall student body. Moreover, they completed fewer hours per term (McDonald, 1981).

A number of reasons were given for the lack of success: pressures from home to fulfill family obligations, the competitive environment of higher education institutions, weak academic backgrounds, lack of supportive counseling or academic remediation, and culture shock were cited in related research (Eschwage, 1971). As a result of a number of studies there was increased awareness among Indian leaders that existing higher education did not meet the needs of people at the reservation level (McDonald, 1981).

The late 1960s and early 1970s, as for the United States as a whole, was a time of great ferment in Indian education. Indians, as well as non-Indian government officials, felt strongly that Indian education required radical changes if improvement was ever to take place. One of these changes was the returning of more control of education and other governmental programs to people at the local level (Adams, 1974). Part of the basis for the movement was simply the lack of educational achievement for Indians shown in statistics (Eder and Reyhner, 1989). In response to such pressures the Secretary of the Interior announced that "by the end of 1975 at least one-fourth of the BIA schools will operate under the management system chosen by those served by the school" (Benham, 1974).

Local control of education and the provision of increased educational opportunities were also addressed by the Indian Education Act, passed by Congress in 1972. This act provided locally controlled, supplementary funds for schools with Indian students; funded Indian students for undergraduate and graduate education in certain fields; and provided local adult education programs (National Advisory Council on Indian Education, 1992).

As a result of factors such as the movement toward return of local educational control and knowledge of the reasons underlying lack of achievement of Indians at off-reservation institutions, the stage was set for the emergence of the tribal college movement (McDonald, 1981). Other factors in the larger environment such as "the civil rights movement; the Johnson administration's War on Poverty; young Indians demanding a better chance at securing the American dream of the good life; and the vision that community colleges could work on Indian reservations" have also been noted as reasons for the movement (Stein, 1988, p. 2).

Navajo Community College, at Many Farms, Arizona, was the first tribal college. A group of enlightened educators and BIA officials on the Navajo Reservation provided leadership for the idea. They believed that education would be key in improving economic life on the reservation. An important concept underlying the curriculum is that the Navajo culture would be its basis. Funding was obtained from tribal, private foundation, and government sources, and classes were first held in January 1969 (Stein, 1988).

An important precedent, which would have great import for the creation of other institutions, was set by Navaho Community College. Based on a belief that education was a treaty right, the Navajo Tribe persuaded their congressional delegation to sponsor financially supportive legislation. As a result, the Navajo Community College Act was passed. The passage of this act gave hope to other reservations that the federal government would lend support for more tribal colleges (Stein, 1988).

During the first half of the 1970s and following the lead of the Navajos, other tribal colleges sprang up. Among these were Standing Rock College, Fort Yates, North Dakota; D-Q University, Davis, California; Oglala Lakota Community College, Pine Ridge, South Dakota; Sinte Gleska College, Rosebud, South Dakota; and Turtle Mountain Community College, Belcourt, North Dakota. In 1972, six of these institutions joined together to create the American Indian Higher Education Consortium (AIHEC), which provided an organization through which the institutions could help one another and consolidate lobbying efforts (McDonald, 1981).

By 1975, Native American tribal groups had chartered and established seven more tribally controlled colleges (Oppelt, 1984). By 1980, there were seventeen tribal colleges in existence (Clifford, 1980). Currently there are twenty-four tribal colleges under the direct control of tribal councils. There are also a number of affiliated institutions, such as the Institute of American Indian Arts (Santa Fe, New Mexico) or Haskell Indian Nations University (Lawrence, Kansas), which are primarily controlled by federal government agencies or boards composed of representatives of many tribal councils.

Difficulties for new and struggling institutions included finding operational funds, suitable classrooms, and qualified faculty. "Tribal colleges had to scramble every year to keep their doors open" (Stein, 1988, p. 6). Financial difficulties were eased somewhat by the passage of the Tribally Controlled Community College Act of 1978 (Wright and Weasel Head, 1990). This act provided grants for the operation and improvement of tribal colleges, technical assistance, and feasibility studies (Public Law 95–471, 95th Congress).

Role and Scope

Although tribal college programs are primarily two years in length, many one-year programs also exist. At least three colleges offer bachelor's degrees and one offers a master's level program. Several others offer the first two years of baccalaureate programs in conjunction with four-year institutions. They have a number of other characteristics in common: location in rural areas on or near geographically isolated Indian reservations or areas of Indian population; boards of directors that are almost exclusively Indian (Wright and Weasel Head, 1990); small student bodies ranging from 100 to 1,200; and surrounding communities that are among the lowest income areas in the United States (One Feather, 1974). Most are located in the western United States and sixteen are situated in three states—Montana, South Dakota, and North Dakota.

These institutions offer a variety of educational opportunities particular to each community and economy. Offerings include vocational education degrees and certificates, paraprofessional and professional degrees, transfer courses, community-interest courses, adult education, and basic literacy programs. Program developers have been careful to create programs that produce graduates with high employability in local markets.

The importance of the transfer function varies from college to college. At many, it is of less importance than the vocational education programs. Tribal administrations have perceived that many Indian students do not aspire to the baccalaureate degree. Many are oriented toward obtaining a skill and going to work as soon as possible.

The independence of the tribal colleges is shown in their adherence to local needs and interests. For example, a few tribal colleges have adamantly stayed with the term scheduling system as opposed to the semester system. Despite difficulties in credit articulation to the many colleges and universities on the semester system, the tribal colleges are determined to give local needs the highest priority.

Relations with mainstream institutions remain cordial. Segments of both institutional types are open to mutually beneficial relationships. A wide spectrum of joint efforts, cooperative agreements, off-campus programs, and other interaction between these institutions and tribal colleges takes place on a regular basis. Illustrative of this is the American Indian Research Opportunities Program at Montana State University, in Bozeman, Montana, which reaches out to all tribal colleges with a newsletter and active recruitment of Indians into their natural sciences programs. Another example is Rocky Mountain College, in Billings, Montana, which heads a consortium of three tribal colleges entitled the Science Alliance Technology Program.

Generally, however, tribal college administration, faculty, and boards believe they can do a better job with the typical Indian student than mainstream colleges. This is part of the reason for a movement toward offering complete baccalaureate and graduate programs. Salish Kootenai College, in Pablo, Montana, for example, has just begun offering its second baccalaureate program in environmental studies. Their first bachelor's-level program was in Human Services. Additionally, Standing Rock College, Fort Yates, North Dakota, offers four-year and master's degrees as of Fall 1994, using a statewide interactive video network. The offering of four-year degrees and graduate programs appears to be a trend. It is probable that more tribal colleges will join this trend, especially as the possibilities of distance learning via satellite or fiber-optic phone lines become more widely used.

A large part of what makes tribal colleges unique can be found in their mission statements, which in most cases declare that the tribal culture will be an integral part of curricular offerings (Boyer, 1989). "Tribal colleges view culture as their curricular center" and "reinforce the values of Indian culture" (p. 28). Tribal colleges have changed the nature of the traditional college curriculum to reflect tribal values. Part of the philosophy underpinning the curriculum is that the origin of the educational mission resides in the people themselves.

Janine Windy Boy-Pease (1990), president of Little Big Horn College, at Crow Agency, Montana refers to the source for her institution's curriculum: "Knowledge can come from spending time in prayer and fasting, from the top of a mountain or the river bottoms, or from a small spirit. . . . [We understood] knowledge was vested in all of us throughout the community. . . . We inherited all these ways in which knowledge could be learned whether it is through observation, from listening, from mentoring, or through very, very meticulous study. We inherited a faith in our own scholarship and in the idea of education" (pp. 37–38).

Cultural courses are defined as specifically Indian culture, including tribal languages, and may comprise a substantial part of the entire number of courses offered. Each academic term, typical Native American Studies departments offer cultural courses such as singing, drumming, art, language, Indian literature, Indian images in the media, Indian history, tribal use of plants, porcupine quill work, hide tanning, tepee construction, and beading. Tribal colleges also frequently sponsor one or more powwows throughout the year and often hold traditional encampments during the summer.

Tribal colleges have a relatively unusual type of student body. The majority are Indian, with a plurality of female students ranging from 60 percent to 70 percent (Boyer, 1989). A substantial number are single parents. Many are not educating themselves to leave their homes but plan to live and work on their own reservations (Tucker, 1979). The average age is twenty-seven, and students who are middle-aged and older are not hard to find (Boyer, 1989). Frequently, these students have not performed any academic work since high school and must relearn basic skills (Boyer, 1989). Developmental studies are a substantial part of the tribal college offerings.

Future

The history of Indians in the United States, similar to the history of other peoples, can be separated into positive and negative eras. A negative period, the Allotment Era, extended from 1890 to 1934. Most Indians were confined to reservations with little or no rights as their land base eroded. A more positive era extended from 1934 to 1945 when Indians found work under social help programs, stabilized their land base and many nations elected to write constitutions. From 1945 to 1968, the Termination Era, the cycle again turned negative as the federal government tried to end treaty obligations with the Indian nations. Six tribes were terminated during this period. In 1970, Richard Nixon announced a government policy more acceptable to Indian nations—self-determination. In large part, despite lukewarm support from the Reagan and Bush administrations, the policy has been to allow Indian nations to control their own destiny as much as possible.

Given this cycle, aware college administrators know that much of their destiny depends on the federal government's interpretation of obligations to honor treaties. Nevertheless, few colleges have taken the opportunity to develop endowment funds that may keep their colleges in operation should hard times return. All tribal colleges would agree that the future of their institutions is tied closely to the intentions of the United States to fulfill treaty obligations regarding education.

Should funding remain steady or grow incrementally, tribal colleges will grow. This growth will take place on two fronts. First the existing tribal colleges will continue to serve more and more Indian students. Most have experienced 5 percent to 10 percent annual growth in their student bodies. In 1993, in Montana, seven young tribal colleges served over 2,000 Indian students while fourteen units of the Montana University System served only 900.

The second type of growth of tribal colleges will occur as other reservations and areas of Indian population push legislators and the BIA to allow them to establish their own tribal colleges. While there are presently twenty-four colleges, there are many more reservations and areas of Indian population that would like to have one. No doubt, some will be able to wield the political power to win this struggle. How many is unknown. A low projection based on applications to AIHEC is that three more will join the ranks before the turn of the century.

No matter what shape the growth curve for tribal colleges takes, the onrush of new technologies (such as interactive video and telecommunications) is also an uncertainty for tribal colleges. Only a few of the institutions have the expertise and resources to ride this steady wave of change. Some will lag far behind, unable to fully participate and offering outdated technologies. An example of the disparity is shown by one northwestern tribal college whose faculty and staff are fully integrated into the Internet communications system. Additionally, they are near to implementing distance learning using interactive compressed videos. At other tribal colleges, though, the typical situation is that few faculty or staff have computers connected to the Internet or a local area network.

One of the reasons for these inconsistencies is funding. Many (if not most) tribal colleges neither have the funding nor perceive the need to invest in what they see as a luxury. Additionally, and equally important, many are wary. They believe technology will hinder the personal relationship between teacher and students that is a hallmark of the type of instruction under which Indians learn best.

Inclination of administrations and faculty notwithstanding, it is more often the better-situated tribal colleges in terms of finance that have the capacity to implement new technology. Unless special measures are taken, signs seem to indicate that the gap will grow between the connected and unconnected. Certain tribal colleges, located in areas of great poverty, need help to finance technological upgrades. This help may come from either government or private sources, but it is vitally needed if tribal colleges are to stay current with computer technology. In order to have the best effect, these funding sources should be sensitive to the ambiguous attitude of some tribal colleges toward technological advances; these institutions do not want to change successful practices of close personal teacher-student interaction. Too great a reliance on computer-assisted instruction may be seen as too remote and detached to be effective with Native American students. In spite of a cool reception by some, however, overall technological advances are seen as inevitable and an enhancement to the mission. A promising development in this field is the acquisition of a U.S. Department of Commerce grant by AIHEC to connect all the tribal colleges with uplink and downlink capabilities.

Tribal colleges appear to be one of the most effective ways to serve Native American educational needs. "They are meeting the unique educational needs of reservation American Indians better than existing institutions of higher education" (Oppelt, 1984, p. 41). Boyer projected that in 1990 over 10,000 full- and part-time students would attend tribal colleges. These colleges serve more Native Americans than any other component of modern postsecondary education (Boyer, 1989, p. 28). A reason for this success is that the educational mission of the colleges directly addresses local needs and interests. These institutions "stand out as the most significant and successful development in Indian education history" (p. 24).

The question still remains, however. Will the tribal colleges be allowed to continue locally planned educational programs that fit their needs as they see them? Tribal colleges need the support of their colleagues in higher education across the country. Not just for a word to their congressional delegations asking for their continued support, although this is certainly important, but for technical assistance in areas of instruction, access to technology, and opportunities to participate in professional organizations. Lastly, tribal colleges ask for understanding. Their cleaving to their specific cultures may be seen as limiting and shortsighted by some, but this adherence is driven by a simple fact— self-esteem and empowerment arises from pride in origin and the degree to which people cherish their heritage. In the end, Indian nations only want what they had 150 years ago and what other more powerful nations have been able to defend—the right to decide for themselves what kind of education their people will receive.

References

Adams, D. "Self-Determination and Indian Education." *Journal of American Indian Education,* 1974, *13* (12), 21.

"Annual Report of the Commissioner of Indian Affairs for 1887." In *House Executive Document No. 1.* Part 5, Vol. II, 50th Congress, 1st session, pp. 18–23. Washington, D.C.: U.S. Government Printing Office, 1987.

Beck, P. V., and Walters, A. L. *The Sacred: Ways of Knowledge, Sources of Life.* Tsaile, Ariz.: Navajo Community College Press, 1977.

Benham, W. J. "A Brief Overview of a Changing Era." *American Indian Education Journal,* 1974, *14* (1), 1.

Boyer, E. *Tribal Colleges Shaping the Future of Native America.* Princeton, N.J.: Carnegie Foundation for the Advancement of Teaching, 1989.

Clark, R. O., "Higher Education Programs for American Indians." *American Indian Education Journal,* 1972, *12* (1), 16–20.

Clifford, L. *About the American Indian Higher Education Consortium.* Denver: American Indian Higher Education Consortium, 1980.

Dobyns, H. F. *Their Number Become Thinned.* Knoxville: University of Tennessee Press, 1983.

Eder, J., and Reyhner, J. *A History of Indian Education.* Billings: Eastern Montana College, 1989.

Eschwage, H. *The Bureau of Indian Affairs Should Do More to Help Educate Indian Students.* Washington, D.C.: U.S. General Accounting Office, 1971. (HRD-77–155)

Fritz, H. E. *The Movement for Indian Assimilation, 1860–1890.* Philadelphia: University of Pennsylvania Press, 1963.

McDonald, J. "An Assessment of Accreditation Practices in Developing Indian Colleges Compared with Non-Indian Community Colleges in the Northwest." Unpublished doctoral dissertation, University of Montana, Missoula, 1981.

McLuhan, T. C., *Touch the Earth: A Self-Portrait of Indian Existence.* New York: Simon & Schuster, 1971.

National Advisory Council on Indian Education. *Indian Education: A Federal Entitlement.* 19th Annual Report to U.S. Congress for Fiscal Year 1992. Washington, D.C.: National Advisory Council on Indian Education, 1992.

One Feather, G. "American Indian Community College." In V. Deloria, Jr. (ed.), *Indian Education Confronting the Seventies: Future Concerns.* Vol. 5. Oglala, S.D.: American Indian Resource Associates, 1974. (ED 113 092)

Oppelt, J. "The Tribally Controlled Colleges in the 1980s: Higher Education's Best Kept Secret." *American Indian Culture and Research Journal,* 1984, *8* (4), 27–45.

Pratt, R. H. *Battlefield and Classroom: Four Decades with the American Indian, 1867–1904.* New Haven, Conn.: Yale, 1964.

Stein, W. J. "A History of the Tribally Controlled Community Colleges: 1968–1978." Unpublished dissertation, Washington State University, Pullman, 1988.

Tucker, S. "Higher Education Outline." Paper presented to the Committee on Education and Labor, U.S. House of Representatives, 1979.

Windy Boy-Pease, J. "Learning in the Social Environment: A Crow Perspective." In R. A. Fellenz and G. Conti (eds.), *Social Environment and Adult Learning.* Bozeman: Center for Adult Learning, Montana State University, 1990.

Wright, B., and Weasel Head, P. "Tribally Controlled Community Colleges: A Student Outcomes Assessment of Associate Degree Recipients." *Community College Review,* 1990, *18* (3), 29–32.

MICHAEL J. HILL is director of institutional research at Salish Kootenai College in Pablo, Montana.

The rural context and the place of women and minorities are presented and analyzed, along with some suggestions regarding issues where change is needed.

Women and Minorities in Rural Community Colleges: Programs for Change

Rosemary Gillett-Karam

Today, the rural United States is known by a set of identifiers that include the words low, slow, and high—low population density, low total populations, low per capita income, low levels of educational attainment, slow job growth, high poverty, high unemployment, and high rates of illiteracy.

This was not always so. As a nation, our history is steeped in a strong identity with rural life. Jefferson's ideal for his country—the yeoman farmer, the work ethic, and grass-roots politics—is made up of idealized rural images. Folkways and mores are tied to rural traditions. From this tradition, there is emerging a growing concern over the need to reacquire our old habits (Bellah, 1985), including especially a strong sense of community self-help. Unfortunately, what is not wanted, necessarily, is to reacquire these habits *in the* rural areas of our country. While charmed by the remembrance of rural life, the rural parts of the country continue to decline. Glossed over is the need to carefully examine the shifting patterns of modern life in rural areas and the critical economic and educational needs there.

Modern economic conditions in rural areas are bleak. The local, self-sufficient farm, never a reality for the entire population, has been replaced by agribusiness. Sharecropping, potentially a venue for farm ownership, has been diminished. The migrant worker has virtually replaced the sharecropper. Company town businesses, such as the mills or canneries, have all but disappeared from most rural communities. Cottage industry, long the major source of wages for rural women, has been displaced by competing world markets. In largely rural states such as those found in the South, half of all white women earn less than $10,700 yearly; half of all Latino, African-American, and Native American

New Directions for Community Colleges, no. 90, Summer 1995 © Jossey-Bass Inc., Publishers

women earn less than $8,000 yearly (Rubin, 1994). In North Carolina, for example, only three percent of all African-American women and 7 percent of white women earn an income above $30,000 (compared to 25 percent of white males).

According to the economists, the proportion of the rural population that lives in poverty is significantly higher than in urban areas. Who are the rural poor? Women, children, the aged, and the minorities are the rural populations who are living in the most desperate poverty. This fact is not new; it has been obvious for many decades, and while there are programs that attempt to address the issue, little progress has been made to alleviate the problems or conditions of poverty. Not only do women or minorities not have jobs (unemployment is significantly higher in rural areas than in urban areas, for the most part); but the jobs they do have pay disproportionately low salaries.

Special Needs for Training and Education

Training and education needs are not keeping pace with the growing needs of a rural population in transition. In the paragraphs that follow, the problems of inaccessibility to rural institutions by migrant workers is discussed; the needs of economic inequality and lack of adequate child and elder care and transportation needs for women are presented; the history of educational discrimination for certain populations is given; and finally, some of the immediate educational needs of rural communities are listed. Other issues are also presented, including leadership discrepancies, need for financial aid, eroding programs for remedial and literacy education, and noninclusive curricula.

Migrant Farmworkers. Latinos, whose populations are concentrated in the Southwest and Florida, are also found in substantial numbers in rural areas—they are distributed along the pathways of the migrant worker. Patterns of the migrant farm worker have been emerging since the early 1960s when news journalist Edward R. Murrow presented the televised documentary on migrant farmworkers, *Harvest of Shame.* Usually, Latino workers are temporary farm laborers, often returning to urban centers that cannot support them (80 percent of Latino farm workers' origins are urban centers in the United States). As migrant farm workers, they bring an average of 6.5 intergenerational family workers with them. They work for a few months and move to new rural areas. Because they are migrant workers, they have no permanent roots; all are needed to work at the low wages they earn, and therefore, few attend school. If they are ill or have a grievance, although they are U.S. citizens, they have no place to go. Access to institutions—for schooling, for hospital care, for legal rights—is limited.

Women's Needs. Women constitute over half the U.S. rural population. Although economists suggest that rural culture is shifting around the nature of rural work, women in rural areas are still characterized by the myth of traditional roles in their communities: Men do the hard farm work and women clean and cook and raise children, and they stay home. Ma and Pa Kettle may not be Ozzie and Harriet, but they share the woman-at-home myth (Coontz, 1992). Even in the examples demonstrating the entrepreneurial inventiveness of rural women (few as they are), women who work continue to have problems related to the need for transportation and child care. Probably the most inventive work rural women do is still tied to home-based industry, and these industries and their piecework are in danger of closing down because of world market competition. It is difficult to know where to begin addressing the issues of women and their work. Women throughout the country must work. If they do work in the rural United States, their wages are substandard and their work is usually low-level (maids, clerks, hairdressers, and waitresses). Moreover, there are virtually no child care facilities in rural areas (Schulman, 1990). The condition of children and the aged parents of rural women remain the purview of the women themselves—and these two populations are the poorest of the poor. Rural women need and want greater access to training but they also need and want child and elder care and transportation.

Minorities and Educational Needs. The history of African-Americans, from 1619 to 1865, almost 250 years, is one of slavery. As property of white masters, economic independence was not possible, nor was school. Unlike African-Americans, Native Americans saw some early attempts for higher education even in colonial times, but for the most part they were treated separately from white populations for schooling. After the 1830s and the aftermath of a long series of Indian wars, those Indians who were left lived on reservations as captive populations. After the Civil War, some schooling was made available to these populations but this was usually provided by churches and volunteers (Montgomery, 1993). Where education was considered a function of the government, as with the separated Indian populations on reservations, boarding schools—whose main purpose was to resocialize Indians—were established. For the most part, schooling and training, were not available to these populations. And although there are examples of African-Americans or Indians in higher education, these examples are few; schools, colleges, and universities were not integrated until the 1940s and 1950s (see Supreme Court decisions in Texas, Oklahoma, Missouri, and Maryland; *Brown* v. *Board of Education,* 1954, in Gillett-Karam, Roueche, and Roueche, 1991, pp. 92–96). It does not come as a surprise, therefore, that researchers continue to report overall declines in the number of African-Americans and Native American Indians in higher education (Carter and Wilson, 1994; Orfield and Ashkinaze, 1991). Limited access to education, especially higher education, despite the courts' rejection of discriminatory policy, continues as an issue for minority populations. Limited access to education in rural areas is exacerbated by cultural traditions that are demonstrated by the lower numbers of these populations either graduating from high school or attending college.

Educational Needs in Rural Communities. In rural areas in the United States, as many as one out of five citizens may have as little as five years of education, and therefore their skills, especially in a job market that is more and more dependent on a smart workforce, are minimal. Illiteracy is a continuing, large problem. In rural areas, it is about ten times harder to find college grad-uates than in urban areas. And because of the proliferation of institutions of higher education, those who do have professional degrees are attracted to teaching and professorial jobs that pay more—and those jobs are in urban areas. There is an overall difficulty of attracting and keeping faculty at every educational level in rural areas, period. Local faculty pools, practically nonex-istent in the past, continue to be low today. Also, very small numbers of fac-ulty are Latino, African-American, or Indian. Women's numbers as faculty are usually consistent with numbers in urban colleges.

Other Issues. These are a few of the particular problems and issues con-fronting rural communities and their female and minority populations. In addi-tion, the more commonly discussed problems and obstacles for these populations also continue, including diminished pathways to leadership posi-tions, difficulties in obtaining financial aid, eroding programs for remedial edu-cation, and noninclusive and nonfunctional curricula. Higher education in general and community colleges specifically have not adequately addressed the needs of rural communities; they have particularly neglected to address the issues that affect a substantial portion of their service area populations—those of women and minorities.

According to a study in a four-state area in the southeastern United States, colleges still claim to be surprised there is less of a pool of students to draw from in rural areas; they remain discouraged about low enrollments and low per capita income (lowering the tax bases for potential use by rural community colleges); they are uncertain about the relationship between the commu-nity and the community college (including the business relationship); and they are unsure about what to do to address high rates of illiteracy (Gillett-Karam and Killacky, 1994). The time has come for colleges to examine and debate these issues and to plan for change. This may not occur without rancor; opin-ions on how to resolve rural educational problems vary and are controversial.

The Debate

Scholars, politicians, and citizens have debated equity issues for community colleges for decades. They are adamant that they do not want to discriminate when making rules among types of U.S. community colleges. Rules, they say, should be standard for all colleges. Thus, full-time equivalencies (FTEs) become the basis for funding for all community colleges—rates are established by the actual number of students attending and remaining in classes. But con-sider this—by using FTEs to drive funding, it is absolutely a fact that rural colleges will have less money. If tax bases are used to raise money for colleges, rural colleges will have less money. If business and industry are depended on for foundation support, rural colleges will have less money. Rural does mean less.

Rural colleges have less money, have a smaller pool of faculty, and have a smaller base from which to recruit students. Because of the economic realities of rural life, students have less ability to pay tuition, transportation, and child care costs—all needs associated with the adult learner. It is true, of course, that rural areas have their share of rich people—but even their wealth (considerable as it may be) cannot balance out the poverty of most of the rural population. Other traditional sources of funding, such as those coming from business and industry, have a minimal effect on increasing money for community colleges because relatively few businesses and industries are located in rural areas. They do not locate in rural areas because of low levels of education and training, and because of other poor conditions encountered in rural communities; thus the cycle of *less* continues. Perhaps by examining the political-historical context of change, a pathway for reform may emerge.

Context for Change

In democracies, there is an expectation of fairness and tolerance. In other words, when the people rule, they may examine the rules and the equal applicability of rules to all people. Consideration of rules implies the rights of one may not infringe on the rights of others. The United States is a nation that is careful about rights, especially individual rights. The hegemony of individual rights over government rights is fundamental to our democracy; this norm explains our basic belief in the dignity, worth, and respect of the individual.

Often both individuals and groups have tested this principle of fairness before the law—seeking justice and equality. Laws are expected to be inclusive of all groups, even competing ones. It is the nature of the system that competitiveness of groups is met through voting, the development of policy, and the meting out of justice through the court system. And as Solomon (1990) suggests, there is also the spirit of the law, which is based on compassion. The law of compassion is derived from the philosophers who ask individuals to care for one another in order to enhance their own society and the common good.

The political history of the United States is characterized by an expanding understanding of the compassionate nature of the law. At times, the law has been more exclusive than inclusive; it has determined who could vote and who could not, who could own property and who could not, who was a citizen and who was not, and who could go to school and who could not. As a nation we have been narrow-minded about the privilege of skin color and gender and geography. This has meant that certain groups in society and certain geographic areas were afforded more rights than others. And usually it has meant that the burden of reclaiming rights fell on those who were excluded.

Equal representation continues to be a goal to strive for, whether in politics, business, or education. There simply are fewer women and minorities represented in these areas than there are white men. Nowhere in organizations are the numbers of these populations equivalent to their population distribution. While many decry the idea of a quota system, they do not see that when an occupation is dominated by 100 percent of an exclusive group that a quota system is in effect. While many in government and business and education debate the idea of special privilege for an emerging group in our society, they forget the privilege that got them where they are. Privilege, today, seems to favor urban populations at the expense of rural populations. Representation is a right of all of us regardless of gender, race, or location.

At the present time, researchers in the community college and in higher education suggest changes that should be instituted to include more women and minorities at every level of higher education (Gillett-Karam, 1992; Richardson and Bender, 1987). Colleges are exhorted to recruit more African-American, Asian, Native American, and Latino faculty and students; they are encouraged to cast their nets wider for purposes of inclusion and representativeness. Colleges are reminded of the need for more women and minorities in positions of leadership. All over the country, colleges are predominately led by white males (89 percent), according to Vaughan, Mellander, and Blois (1994). Equity is also an issue for community colleges. Issues such as sex, age, and cultural disparity, inclusive curricula, varying learning styles, and workplace and classroom harassment are issues needing further scrutiny by community colleges. Into this array of critical problems, the special issues and needs of the rural community college must be added.

Change Agents

The examination of issues and needs should be a shared community and community college goal. Together—using the skills of collaboration (Gray, 1989), consensus, and coalition building—diverse community groups, agencies, institutions, and leaders can work for change. Kanter describes *change masters* (1984) as those agents of society who perform environmental scans, who seek to understand the conditions of the environment on individuals and their organizations, and who collectively represent the resources of the separate agencies and organizations they represent. Gray (1989) suggests these individuals are the *stakeholders,* members of groups and organizations who have a stake in the outcome of an issue. Stakeholders point to a shared vision, consensus, and collaboration around issues as the means to avoid conflict and stagnation. If community colleges and their communities work together, they may become catalysts for community problem solving. Together they are cast in the roles of change agents, stakeholders, and representatives in order to address the collective problems of their communities.

To this association of community agents must be added a more extensive stakeholder and representative constituency. Boards of trustees, college presidents and their councils, state departments of community colleges, state legislatures, community college personnel, students, and other critical stakeholders need to collaboratively determine what should be done about the issues of higher education in rural communities. This formulation of a committee of representatives of the college, the community, the government, and the business sector is critical for formulating change strategies. This group

needs to work collaboratively as a responsive citizenry and leadership team to design and implement plans of action or programs for individual rural colleges. They may begin by addressing those whom poverty and economic setbacks affect most.

Galbraith (1992) discusses the particular problems of women and minorities in rural community colleges. He says they face economic, personal, interpersonal, community, and institutional obstacles to their success. Moreover, he reports, there are special needs of these populations—for example, the need for nontraditional occupations and nontraditional careers that could transform their lives. There are the less-visible problems, too. Rural women and minorities are caught in a cultural bind—there are new ambitions for these groups, such as those publicized by the media and those resulting from trends. At the same time, these groups are living in conservative and traditional areas, where new ambitions seem remote and inappropriate for the culture (Dunne, 1985). Both Galbraith and Dunne suggest new programs emanating from educational institutions may alleviate the special needs these populations have. The community, with the help of its community college and its broader stakeholder groups, can be involved in transformational change—this is the change that deliberately transcends the linear business-as-usual operations of institutions.

Change and Rural Community Development

A strong, representative voice for rural issues, community development, and community change point the way to strong and transformational rural restructuring. Christenson and Robinson (1984) demonstrate that development implies improvement, growth, and change—it is concerned with the transition of cultures, societies, and communities. Development as improvement focuses on social transformation. Development as growth involves economic and technological transformation. And development as change involves restructuring patterns and policies already in place.

Warren further defines community development as "a process of helping community people analyze their problems, to exercise as large a measure of autonomy as is possible and feasible, and to promote a greater identification of the individual citizen and the individual organization with the community as a whole" (1978, p. 20). The community development involves a group of people in a particular community who collaboratively reach a decision to initiate a social action process to change their economic, social, cultural, or environmental situation—it is, in short, a purposeful attempt to improve communities under the democratic conditions of participation (Phifer, 1980, p. 19).

Community change suggests a process for community and community college participation and collaboration around community issues. Analyzing the needs in communities, the community college acts as a neutral catalyst to bring together those actors who can specifically identify issues that need immediate and long-range resolution. Imperative to the resolution of issues, how-

ever, is the recognition and inclusion of the populations whose quality of life is most affected. If issues of the rural community include child and elder care, transportation of individuals to educational institutions, access to hospitals and legal institutions, and the need for higher educational training for jobs, then representatives work together to develop and implement plans and policies to address these issues. Resources are generated from people, agencies, and organizations working together to resolve the issue and to continue to examine and readjust its impact. The following suggestions for rural change are offered for consideration.

Suggestions for Rural Change and Educational Transformation

Rural communities, their colleges, and their representatives need to recognize and respond to the conditions and needs of women, African-Americans, Indians, and Latinos in their communities. Economic and educational needs account for the majority of their concerns and issues. The following suggestions offer beginning points for the representatives of change to analyze, plan, and develop programs. The first few suggestions are general ones, the last suggestions address specific educational issues.

1. Economic development is critical for rural communities and rural community colleges can lead the way for expanded development. By establishing local economic development joint ventures, local community government and community colleges can begin to examine the special needs of the community and monitor the changing needs of businesses and workers. Rural colleges can be very active in addressing the workplace training of local business and industry; they are an excellent magnet for business and industry locations. State systems should provide an economic development office in each community college in the state. If the products of the workers are in jeopardy from international competition (like the piecework of women in rural areas), this is a problem for examination by representatives of the community change agents—measures that are adopted for economic stability are critical for rural communities.

2. Collaborative efforts, through intergovernmental and interagency agreements, can be developed to address educational needs. Average education levels should be monitored and disseminated as indicators for growth and development. Efforts should be made to understand educational needs in context; literacy needs are an example. Illiteracy should be equated with crime and poverty in terms of urgency. Since various agencies deal with literacy problems in any given geographic location, it makes good sense that collaborative efforts profit the recipients. Tracking for continuing enrollment in educational institutions can be more easily monitored. Attention is focused on gathering data to indicate the successes of growing literate populations in rural areas.

3. Information and its distribution is undergoing a major revolution through the use of personal computers. Information highways, linkages among

institutions—hospitals, governments, schools, and colleges—are possible and are already in some states active. The idea of computer services to rural areas, as it unfolds, is simply amazing. It offers a means to bring educators and education from all over the country and the world to anyone who has telephone capability and computer access, and where telephones are not part of the household, colleges can provide students with access to the information highway. The information highway idea addresses issues such as how to overcome limited numbers of faculty and limitations on faculty pools in rural areas of the United States. It can also provide home, and interactive, settings for training and earning degrees. Technology is a critical means for adjusting for the educational needs of rural Americans. Good faith and early efforts should be made to provide technological resources to rural communities.

4. State legislatures initially, and local taxing agencies eventually, should examine and consider a progressive rating of geographical localities, rather than a regressive one, to determine funding for rural community colleges. Instead of treating all equally, state legislatures should account for the differences in per capita and business income for rural community colleges and add a dimension of funding to rural colleges to attract more teachers, to develop additional courses that address educational and training needs, to increase the technical-vocational preparation for students for the new workforce, to seek transportation and child care facilities for students, to aid in tuition payments, and to encourage partnerships among elementary schools, junior and senior high schools, and community colleges.

5. Rural communities and community colleges need to question just how difficult it is to find postbaccalaureate faculty, and how impossible it is to find women and minorities to fill leadership positions in community colleges. Programs that add incentives to faculty salaries in rural areas should be instituted. Programs to educate local members of communities for postbaccalaureate degrees should be initiated. In times of dwindling resources, local industries and businesses can mentor local students, and provide them with money for graduate school in return for their promise to return to the community to work and to teach.

6. Rural community colleges particularly need to examine and reexamine student transfer and success rates, and to determine if those students who are successfully transferring have incentives to return to the community to lead the battle for parity and equity for future generations. One suggestion is for colleges to begin immediately to teach and develop leadership skills for students. Another suggestion is for colleges to make curriculum more relevant and inclusive for diverse populations. None of these things will ensure student return without adequate jobs, however.

7. Community college counselors and special community college courses, especially in continuing education, can point the way for new discussions and new careers for rural populations. Special efforts need to be made to avoid pigeonholing rural students, and special efforts should be underway to counsel students to the needs of the new workforce and the rapidly changing

culture. Expanding careers for women should be a routine part of college services. Colleges must be active recruiters of underrepresented populations, especially members of racial and ethnic minorities. Mentoring programs are critical to these populations.

8. For transient populations, community colleges need to make efforts to take education to the migrant worker and to assure these workers that they have a place to bring their questions and concerns. Outreach programs can aid migrant workers to understand legal aid and hospital services that are available to them.

9. Child care must become the collective responsibility of the community and the community college. While these centers are expensive, colleges may find resources in cooperative arrangements with businesses and from elderly citizens who are no longer active in the workforce. Transportation is also a critical problem for many of the students in rural areas. By assessing student needs and arrangement of classes, ride-sharing opportunities may become a feature of college services.

10. Every effort should be made to promote women and minorities into community college leadership positions, including the presidency, the vice-presidency, and the dean levels of administration, and to boards of trustees.

Conclusion

In summary, rural communities and community colleges should be working together with other stakeholders and representatives to resolve the issues affecting their economic and educational quality of life. Positive developmental programs should address the special needs of rural populations. While perhaps cures for the social issues incurred by poverty may not be easily eliminated, immediate need issues can be actively and aggressively addressed. The challenge ahead is to demonstrate that the needs of rural populations in the United States are contextual to the whole of our society—without solutions to the lows, and slows, and highs of economic and educational indicators, the whole United States suffers. Rural community colleges are called upon to become beacons for economic and educational change, and as they demonstrate this for their own communities, they demonstrate it for us all.

References

Bellah, R. *Habits of the Heart: Individualism and Commitment in American Life.* New York: HarperCollins, 1985.
Carter, D., and Wilson, R. *Minorities in Education.* Washington, D.C.: American Council on Education, 1994.
Christenson, J., and Robinson, E. "Gemeinshaft and Gesellschaft." *Social Forces,* 1984, *63* (1), 77–80.
Coontz, S. *The Way We Never Were.* New York: Basic Books, 1992.
Dunne, F. *Education in Rural America.* Boulder, Colo.: Westview Press, 1985.
Galbraith, M. W. (ed.). *Education in the Rural American Community: A Lifelong Process.* Malabar, Fla.: Krieger, 1992.

Gillett-Karam, R. "Confronting Diversity in the Community College Classroom." In K. Kroll (ed.), *Maintaining Faculty Excellence*. New Directions for Community Colleges, no. 79. San Francisco: Jossey-Bass, 1992.

Gillett-Karam, R., and Killacky, J. "Pathways to Tomorrow: A Conversation about Community-Based Programming." *Journal of the Community Development Society*, 1994, 25 (1), 111–122.

Gillett-Karam, R., Roueche, S., and Roueche, J. *Underrepresentation and the Question of Diversity: Women and Minorities in the Community College*. Washington, D.C.: Community College Press, 1991.

Gray, B. *Collaborating: Finding Common Ground for Multiparty Problems*. San Francisco: Jossey-Bass, 1989.

Kanter, R. *The Change Masters*. New York: Simon & Schuster, 1984.

Montgomery, W. *Under Their Vine and Fig Tree*. Baton Rouge: Louisiana State University Press, 1993.

Orfield, G., and Ashkinaze, C. *The Closing Door*. Chicago: University of Chicago Press, 1991.

Phifer, E. W., Jr. *Burke: The History of a North Carolina County*. Morganton, N.C.: Phifer, 1980.

Richardson, R., and Bender, L. *Fostering Minority Access and Achievement in Higher Education: The Role of Urban Community Colleges and Universities*. San Francisco: Jossey-Bass, 1987.

Rubin, S. *What Is a Woman Worth?* Raleigh, N.C.: North Carolina Equity, 1994.

Schulman, M. *Bringing Up a Moral Child*. New York: Doubleday, 1990.

Solomon, R. *A Passion for Justice*. Reading, Mass.: Addison-Wesley, 1990.

Vaughan, G., Mellander, G., and Blois, B. *The Community College Presidency*. Washington, D.C.: Community College Press, 1994.

Warren, R. *New Perspectives on the American Community*. Skokie, Ill.: Rand McNally, 1978.

ROSEMARY GILLETT-KARAM *is associate professor of higher education, adult and community college education, North Carolina State University at Raleigh.*

Distance education is now a part of the higher education agenda, and this chapter provides examples to illustrate its influence and impact on rural community colleges.

Distance Education: The Way of the Future for Rural Community Colleges

Pamela S. MacBrayne

Demographic shifts, societal changes, and technological advances are rapidly altering the nature of the college student body. During the 1970s, adult learners accounted for almost half the growth in college enrollments. Students aged twenty-five or older comprised 38 percent of college enrollment in 1977 and 42 percent in 1987 (National Center for Education Statistics, 1988). In the same study it was predicted that adults would account for more than 45 percent of college enrollment by 1997. Female enrollment in college has also been increasing, rising from 39 percent of total enrollment in 1965 to 51 percent in 1985 (McDaniels, 1989).

Many institutions of higher education are experiencing or considering change in response to the diverse needs of these adult students. It is difficult, however, to restructure an institution when its curriculum, services, scheduling, physical facilities, budgets, and staff were developed for the traditional student. Consequently, there is often an awkward fit between the institution and those adult students who increasingly require access to continuing education.

Developed primarily during the past hundred years, U.S. educational institutions were designed for a population that was young and in need of preparation for life in an industrial economy. In Western society, educational institutions are now faced with the problem of a declining pool of the eighteen to twenty-one-year-old students they were originally founded to serve. At the same time, they are challenged by the increasing demand from adults requiring a variety of educational opportunities to prepare them for the postindustrial society. Most of these adults have jobs, personal interests, and family responsibilities that limit their college attendance to part-time. Thus, they do not require dormitories, dining centers, or the same social activities that residential colleges and universities have spent decades developing. It seems clear that these adult students need, instead, convenience in terms of access—evening and weekend courses, ample parking, faculty, services, and offices available at appropriate times—and an educational delivery system that takes into account the realities of life of a busy adult who may not have the time, inclination, or financial resources to commute long distances (Connick and MacBrayne, 1988).

Community colleges have led the way in accommodating the needs of adult learners and providing the services required to ensure their success. The difficulty of meeting the needs of on-campus adults is compounded when trying to serve adult students in rural areas who live at some distance from the campus and are unable either to commute or to leave home, work, and family to live in a college dormitory. In rural areas of the United States there are fewer educational institutions, opportunities, and resources than in urban areas. Access is often limited because of poor public transportation, the adult learners' geographic isolation, and the lack of a comprehensive education delivery system (Aslanian, cited in Treadway, 1984). Yet rural community colleges have a special role in providing access for the adults in their region, as often they are the only institution located nearby.

One early strategy for educational delivery to those separated geographically from educational institutions was the use of correspondence courses and courses by newspaper and radio. Later, some rural community colleges implemented extension campuses or off-campus centers; either campus faculty would travel to these remote locations, or local, part-time instructors were employed. Now, an increasing number of rural community colleges are responding to the growing number of adults who need higher education by providing programs of distance education that utilize electronic telecommunications technologies for communication between faculty and students.

Technological, Demographic, and Societal Shifts

Much has been written regarding the significant and rapid changes affecting the structure of contemporary society and our lives within that society. Authors such as Toffler (1980) and Naisbitt (1984) have produced widely read works that describe these changes and predict their influence on the future. In recent years, mechanical power has been widely replaced by electronic power, allowing us to perform both physical and mental activities with relative ease and blinding speed. This has resulted in the rapid development and accumulation of information and knowledge.

Approximately 55 percent of the current workforce in the United States is employed in information industries. As Johnson (1984) points out, "Yesterday's futuristic prophecies—the electronic office, the automated factory, the computerized household—are rapidly becoming today's realities. Work demands verbal and quantitative competencies, perhaps requiring total retraining and recertification of many workers to smooth the transition to a technology-based society" (p. 72).

The exponential growth of information and knowledge is one of the most exciting but confounding aspects of life in modern society. As educational institutions attempt to deal with this expansion of knowledge, they encounter the challenge of revising old curricula, designing new programs, and developing new delivery mechanisms to continually educate an increasing number of people.

Demographic changes have resulted in an increased number of adults between the ages of twenty-five and forty-five relative to other age groups. This shift in the population is a result of the aging of the "baby boom" cohort and a decrease in the birthrate. In addition, as Hodgkinson (1986) reports, in 1983 there were, for the first time in the history of the United States, more people over the age of sixty-five than teenagers. This shift to an older population has implications for many facets of life, including education.

Other social changes, such as the altered roles of women and men, earlier retirement, increased leisure time, changing lifestyles, increased educational attainment of the populace, and new career opportunities have also influenced greatly the growth in lifelong learning. The growth in the percentage of women in the workforce parallels the growth of women enrolled in college. According to McDaniels (1989), females accounted for 33.4 percent of the workforce in 1960 and 45.8 percent in 1990.

Furthermore, it is predicted that one-half of all jobs that exist today will not exist in the year 2000. Those jobs will be replaced by others requiring new skills based on significantly increased educational levels and, consequently, greater access to education (Connick and MacBrayne, 1988). McDaniels (1989) reports that the projections show growth in the proportion of jobs requiring at least one year of college, a slight decline in the share of jobs requiring a high school diploma and a sharp decline in the share of jobs requiring less than a high school education. Naisbitt (1982) suggested that the workers of tomorrow will need more brainpower and less brawn power if they are to function effectively in the new work settings.

Development of Distance Education

Correspondence education is considered the forerunner of distance education in the United States, having been actively used for over 150 years. Although the first significant correspondence effort in North America was the Chautauqua movement, the first documented correspondence education occurred in Boston in 1728 (Holmberg, 1986). One of the primary goals of correspondence education was to provide access for those unable to attend traditional classroom instruction, regardless of educational or socioeconomic background. Correspondence courses in the universities tended to be extensions of regular academic courses, taught by regular faculty by means of assigned readings. Students prepared written lessons that were submitted to the instructor and returned with comments. These courses were usually offered on a regular basis, and many universities permitted up to half the courses in a degree program to be taken by correspondence (Knowles, 1962). In addition to access, correspondence provided the first formally structured method of independent study (Wedemeyer, 1981).

Despite its importance, correspondence study has recognized limitations. Information is provided in print, by mail or newspaper, with student responses delivered by mail. This results in relatively slow two-way communication that can frustrate students (Holmberg, 1986). Garrison (1987) reports that motivation is difficult to sustain over time and may explain the relatively high dropout rates in correspondence-based distance education. Consequently, many institutions assign a tutor who is available to answer questions when they arise, not only to sustain motivation but also to counteract the sense of isolation and need for affiliation felt by many correspondence students (Persons and Catchpole, 1987).

Although the concept and practice of distance education are not new, the term itself has become increasingly associated with the use of new technologies (Granger, 1990). According to Verduin and Clark, "While formal distance education has been around at least since the early nineteenth century, the development in recent years of new technologies has led to a growing interest in learning at a distance on the part of adults and continuing educators" (1991, p. 4).

Rumble (1986) describes distance education programs as those characterized by the separation of teacher and student, the provision of two-way communication, and the use of technologies such as computer, telephone, and television. Others, including Keegan (1986), define distance education more broadly, encompassing programs in which communication between learners and teachers is accomplished by print and writing (correspondence) as well as electronically.

The first electronic mechanism used to serve distant learners was instructional radio. Then the initial telecourses appeared with the advent of broadcast television in the 1950s. These telecourses brought traditional classroom presentations to students at home. TV College, an extension of the City Colleges of Chicago, began operations in 1956, with programs being broadcast over Chicago's public educational television station, WTTW. The history of this project reflects the changes that have occurred throughout the country, from the talking-head series used at a single college, to a system of highly developed and integrated video and print instructional materials designed for national distribution (Hudspeth and Brey, 1985).

Some telecourses include microcomputer exercises as well (Gripp, 1977). Instructional radio and telecourses, however, retain some of the shortcomings of correspondence. Two-way communication is limited and slow, and students sometimes feel isolated. Furthermore, the development of telecourses can take up to three years, resulting in dated materials (Hudspeth and Brey, 1985). Nevertheless, over a million adult learners enrolled in the Adult Learning Services telecourses of the Public Broadcasting Service between 1981 and 1988 (Public Broadcasting Service, 1989).

Audio teleconferencing, which emerged in the 1960s, represented a significant departure from study through correspondence, radio, and broadcast television (Garrison, 1989). Utilizing networks that feature teleconferencing speakers and microphones, students meet in small groups and receive live instruction from a campus-based instructor (Treadway, 1984). This method allows discussion among teachers and students to be carried on simultaneously across wide geographic areas.

Interactive video and computers are a new generation of conferencing. Interactive television overcomes some of the deficiencies of telecourses—students in remote sites can see and hear the instructor and can ask questions using an audio talkback system, thereby eliminating the frustration of delayed responses. Furthermore, local production can incorporate local conditions and areas of interest. Because live interactive television transmits what is happening in the on-campus classroom, the quality of the instruction—good or bad—is the same for all students. Satellite, microwave, cable television, and fiber-optic cable capabilities allow the transmission of audio, video, and data; and their potential for helping distant learners increases daily. These distribution systems are now being used in combination, increasing access for learners who are unable or unwilling to travel to a campus for a course (Hudspeth and Brey, 1985).

With regard to the future of adult education, Brockett and Hiemstra suggest that "the newest efforts at nontraditional degree or study programs involve the development of distance learning through various technologically-assisted delivery models. Television and satellite transmissions, electronic networks, and teleconferencing are some of the forms being developed through experimentation" (1991, p. 161). While audio and video telecommunications have been widely used and acclaimed for their ability to provide instruction to groups of students, the microcomputer is beginning to address the issues of individualization of instruction as well as enhanced communication between faculty and students and among students themselves. The integration of microcomputers and videodiscs provides a powerful interactive educational technology. Garrison (1989) suggests that "distant learners not only will be able to: study when and where they like, but they will be able to choose how they wish to learn and to have all the guidance and support they require or request, thereby acquiring maximum control of the educational transaction" (p. 225).

Davis and Marlow (1986) concur, suggesting that computers and telecommunication networks have enabled learners in remote locations to feel that they are part of larger groups. They believe that the computer reduces isolation, enabling colleagues and learners to make contact and keep in touch with one another.

According to Garrison (1987), "Adult educators must recognize the ability of telecommunications and microprocessor technology to assist adult educators to reach out to adult learners in a variety of settings" (p. 317). Hiemstra and Sisco contend that technological developments are having a significant impact on the ways in which people learn. "The number and type of resources available to learners and educators alike are growing at an astounding rate, primarily because technological developments have speeded up the process of accumulating and disseminating information. . . . Teleconferencing, correspondence study, internships, apprenticeships and a multitude of distance or open learning programs are only some of the nontraditional learning experiences in which adults throughout the world are engaged. In fact, the rapid advance of electronic communication technology suggests that an ever increasing number of adults will be involved with learning in nontraditional settings" (1990, pp. 136–137).

A number of studies have demonstrated that achievement and attitude measured in televised instruction are equivalent or superior to those in face-to-face instruction (Haaland and Newby, 1984; Robertson, 1987; Carver and MacKay, 1986; Silvernail and Johnson, 1987; Shaeffer and Roe, 1985; Johnson, 1990). Some studies, however, report mixed results (Chu and Schramm, 1967; Holt, 1980; Porter, 1983; Denton, 1984). For example, Chu and Schramm (1967) compiled 207 published studies in which television teaching was compared with conventional teaching. Of the 425 separate comparisons, 308 showed no statistically significant differences in student achievement while 67 showed television instruction to be superior and 50 found conventional instruction better.

After a review of the literature, which included more than one hundred published and unpublished documents regarding the effectiveness of televised instruction, Whittington (1986) reported several major findings:

Comparative studies indicate that students taking courses via television achieve, in most cases, as well as students taking courses via traditional methods.

Findings of equivalent student achievement hold even when rigorous methodological research standards are applied.

Television is a technological device for transmitting communication and has no intrinsic effect, for good or ill, on student achievement.

Effective instructional design and techniques are the crucial elements in student achievement whether instruction is delivered by television or by traditional means.

In addition, an evaluation of the Community College of Maine, prepared by Johnson (1990), reported no significant differences with regard to grades between students in the remote classrooms and those in the on-campus studio classroom. After reviewing an array of materials on program quality and effectiveness, Verduin and Clark concluded: "Distance education methodology appears to achieve cognitive outcomes equal to those achieved by the more traditional means of education delivery for adults. In many cases the scale even tips toward distance education. Distance education can also be effective when considering affective and psychomotor outcomes" (1991, p. 117). They go on to suggest that all of this information should allay some of the concerns and suspicions of educators who question this mode of delivery for adults.

In addition to examining learner outcomes, Verduin and Clark (1991) reviewed the literature on access, quality, cost effectiveness and efficiency, impact, relevance to needs and generation of knowledge. They concluded that the evidence and discussion favored distance education. Even though the research was generally based in countries other than the United States, they contend that, based on the limited evidence available on programs in the United States, further research would lend similar results.

Technology and Transformation

Today, telecommunications technologies are challenging the fundamental tenets upon which our entire educational system has been constructed. Modern telecommunications allow us to span distances and cultures instantaneously. The need to aggregate people simply to communicate with them has disappeared. We now have the capacity to provide individuals, at locations of their own choosing, with vast, and rapidly expanding, collections of print and visual materials and the means to share limited resources among many educational institutions (Connick and Russo, 1993). The importance of distance education is particularly significant for rural community colleges. It is essential that their students obtain the knowledge and skills needed to compete in an ever-changing, increasingly global economy. Advances in telecommunications allow rural community colleges to serve students in their own communities by providing a broader array of educational resources once available only in larger, cosmopolitan institutions. Students and faculty can be linked together without either having to travel long distances. And information resources are no longer limited to the library collection on one small campus.

Many rural community colleges have discovered the transformation in teaching and learning brought about by advances in information technologies. Some are using technology to bring a broader range of programs to their campus. Others are using technology to reach beyond their campus to teach those previously unserved in their remote communities.

In North Dakota, for example, the small two-year institutions of the University of North Dakota, Lake Region, and the University of North Dakota, Williston, have joined their campuses to share business faculty electronically. In this manner they are able to expand the breadth of curricular offerings to students in both institutions, allowing students access to their differing expertise. In addition, the Lake Region campus sends their Legal Assistant program to Williston, where it would otherwise not be available.

When the legislature of North Dakota (population, 630,000; area, 70,665 square miles) mandated that nurses obtain a bachelor's degree, the University of North Dakota delivered its Nursing Education program to Lake Region and

Williston via interactive television. Graduate courses in education and social work are also delivered.

Further east, the Community College of Maine uses an interactive television system to reach out to more than a hundred communities in an effort to provide access to its population of 1.2 million, dispersed over 30,000 square miles. It offers nearly sixty courses each semester, and over 3,000 students take advantage of the five associate degree programs available electronically.

Conclusion

Despite the benefits of distance education to rural community colleges and the students they serve, implementing such programs is not a simple task. Certain conditions, however, will enhance the chances of success. First, there must be an assessed need for the expansion of access to programs and services. Secondly, providing such access must be integral to the college's mission and a priority of the institutional leadership, the faculty, and the community. Finally, adequate resources must be committed, not only for the acquisition of technology but also for faculty and staff development.

When used appropriately, technologies can clearly enhance the effectiveness of teaching and learning. Rural community colleges are well positioned to be at the forefront of distance education, benefiting the students they are committed to serve. An important planning consideration is for administration and faculty to be keenly aware of the factors that motivate adults to participate in distance learning. That topic is addressed in Chapter Ten.

References

Brockett, R., and Hiemstra, R. *Self-Direction in Adult Learning.* London: Routledge & Kegan Paul, 1991.

Carver, J., and MacKay, R. C. "Interactive Television Brings University Classes to the Home and Workplace." *Canadian Journal of University Continuing Education,* 1986, *115* (1), 19–28.

Chu, G. C., and Schramm, W. *Learning from Television: What the Research Says.* Stanford, Calif.: Institute for Communication Research, 1967.

Connick, G., and MacBrayne, P. *Telecommunications and Educational Access.* Combined Proceedings, Sixth Annual Conference on Interactive Instruction Delivery and Third Annual Conference on Learning Technology in the Health Care Sciences, Society for Applied Learning Technology, Orlando, Fla., Feb. 24–26, 1988.

Connick, G., and Russo, J. Unpublished manuscript, University of Maine, Augusta, 1993.

Davis, B., and Marlow, C. "The Computer as a Networking and Information Resource for Adult Learners." In B. Heermann (ed.), *Personal Computers and the Adult Learner.* New Directions for Continuing Education, no. 29. San Francisco: Jossey-Bass, 1986.

Denton, J. S. "An Examination of Instructional Strategies Used with Two-Way Television." Paper presented at the annual meeting of the American Educational Research Association, New Orleans, 1984. 21 pp. (ED 238 407)

Garrison, D. R. "Researching Dropouts in Distance Education: Some Directional and Methodological Considerations." *Distance Education,* 1987, *8* (1), 95–101.

Garrison, D. R. "Distance Education." In S. Merriam and P. Cunningham (eds.), *Handbook of Adult and Continuing Education.* San Francisco: Jossey-Bass, 1989.

Granger, D. "Open Universities: Closing the Distances to Learning." *Change*, 1990, 22 (4), 44–47, 49–50.

Gripp, T. "Telecourses Have Designs on You." *T.H.E. Journal: Technological Horizons in Education*, 1977, 4, 12–13.

Haaland, B. A., and Newby, W. G. "Student Perception of Effective Teaching Behaviors: An Examination of Conventional and Teleconference-Based Instruction." In L. A. Parker and C. H. Olgren (eds.), *Teleconferencing and Electronic Communications III*. Madison: University of Wisconsin Extension, 1984.

Hiemstra, R., and Sisco, B. *Individualizing Instruction: Making Learning Personal, Empowering, and Successful*. San Francisco: Jossey-Bass, 1990.

Hodgkinson, H. "The Role of the Adult Student in Enrollment Management." *College Board*, Nov. 1986.

Holmberg, B. *Status and Trends of Distance Education*. London: Croom Helm, 1986.

Holt, R. E., Jr. "The Effectiveness of University Television Instruction and Factors Influencing Student Attitudes." *College Student Journal*, 1980, 14 (1), 5–7.

Hudspeth, D., and Brey, R. *Instructional Telecommunications: Principles and Applications*. New York: Praeger, 1985.

Johnson, J. L. *Evaluation Report of the Community College of Maine Instructional Television System*. Portland: University of Southern Maine Testing and Assessment Center, 1990.

Johnson, L. *The High-Technology Connection: Academic/Industrial Cooperation for Economic Growth*. ASHE-ERIC Higher Education Research Report No. 6. Washington D.C.: Association for the Study of Higher Education, 1984.

Keegan, D. *The Foundations of Distance Education*. London: Croom Helm, 1986.

Knowles, M. *The Adult Education Movement in the United States*. Troy, Mo.: Holt, Rinehart & Winston, 1962.

McDaniels, C. *The Changing Workplace: Career Counseling Strategies for the 1990s and Beyond*. San Francisco: Jossey-Bass, 1989.

Naisbitt, J. *Megatrends: Ten New Directions Transforming Our Lives*. New York: Warner Books, 1982.

Naisbitt, J. *Megatrends: Ten New Directions Transforming Our Lives*. (2nd ed.) New York: Warner Books, 1984.

National Center for Education Statistics. *Projections of Education Statistics to 1997–98*. Washington, D.C.: U.S. Department of Education, 1988.

Persons, H., and Catchpole, M. "The Addition of Audio-Teleconferencing to Interactive Telecourses: An Experimental Analysis of Drop-Out Rates." *Distance Education*, 1987, 8, 251–258.

Porter, T. B. "A Closed-Circuit Television Course in Criminal Law." *Improving College and University Teaching*, 1983, 31 (1), 33–36.

Public Broadcasting Service. *PBS Adult Learning Satellite Service*. Alexandria, Va.: Public Broadcasting Service, 1989.

Robertson, B. "Audio Teleconferencing: Low-Cost Technology for External Studies Networking." *Distance Education*, 1987, 8 (1), 121–130.

Rumble, G. *The Planning and Management of Distance Education*. New York: St. Martin's Press, 1986.

Shaeffer, J. M., and Roe, R. G. "Effective Teaching of Behaviors as Perceived by Students in a Face-to-Face and Teleconferencing Course." In L. A. Parker and C. H. Olgren (eds.), *Teleconferencing and Electronic Communication IV*. Madison: University of Wisconsin Extension, 1985.

Silvernail, D. L., and Johnson, J. L. "The Effects of the University of Southern Maine Instructional Television System on Students' Achievements and Attitudes." Paper presented at Technological Advances in Education and Training Conference, University of Maine, Augusta, Oct. 1–2, 1987.

Toffler, A. *The Third Wave*. New York: Morrow, 1980.

Treadway, D. *Higher Education in Rural America: Serving the Adult Learner*. New York: College Entrance Examination Board, 1984.

Verduin, J., and Clark, T. *Distance Education: The Foundation of Effective Practice*. San Francisco: Jossey-Bass, 1991.

Wedemeyer, C. A. *Learning at the Backdoor: Reflections on Non-Traditional Learning in the Lifespan*. Madison: University of Wisconsin Press, 1981.

Whittington, N. I. "Is Instructional Television Educationally Effective? A Research Review." *American Journal of Distance Education*, 1986, (1), 147–157.

PAMELA S. MACBRAYNE is dean of telecommunications and academic development for the University of Maine System, Augusta.

Environmental scanning allows rural community colleges to forecast change, identify implications for the organization, and plan preferred responses to shape the future.

Environmental Scanning Practices for Rural Colleges

Janice Nahra Friedel, Joel D. Lapin

During the last decade, many improbabilities have turned into realities: the elimination of thousands of previously "safe" management and sales jobs in corporations such as IBM and Sears, the collapse of Communism in Eastern Europe and the Soviet Union, genetic manipulation, and the rise of "majority minorities." To say that the world is changing rapidly is passive and worst of all, clichéd. Hallett (1987) describes this period as the "Present Future": A time of rapid and profound change when the need to respond to the challenges of the future exist in the present. The many and complex changes we experience require colleges and universities to move out of a reactive mode of operation to one of anticipation. Colleges need to forecast change, identify its likely implications for the organization, and plan preferred responses to shape the future.

Rural areas are currently at the center of demographic changes that make a compelling case for involvement in external environmental scanning and forecasting on the part of community colleges serving them. In some parts of the country, for example the West and South, traditionally rural areas are experiencing a large influx of new residents from "outside" and more urbanized areas; other rural areas, for example the Mid-Atlantic and Midwest, are losing population, especially their young people. Both demographic changes could have been anticipated and college responses offered if rural community colleges had instituted external environmental scanning and forecasting.

Colleges and the External Environment

Community colleges are heavily influenced by the external environment; monitoring these changes and their potential impact on the institution is a critical component of strategic planning. Environmental scanning is a method that enables decision makers to understand the external environment and to translate this understanding into the institution's planning and decision making processes. "The goal of environmental scanning is to alert decision makers to potentially significant external changes before they crystalize so that the decision maker has sufficient lead time to react to the change" (Morrison, 1992).

Brown and Weiner (cited in Morrison and Held, 1989) define environmental scanning as "a kind of radar to scan the world systematically and signify the new, unexpected, the major and the minor." Further definition is offered by Coates (1986), who indicates that environmental scanning includes detecting scientific, technical, economic, social, and political interactions and other elements important to the organization; defining the potential threats, opportunities, and changes for the organization caused by those events; promoting a futures orientation in management and staff; and, alerting management and staff to trends that are converging, diverging, speeding up, slowing down, or interacting.

By conducting external environmental scanning and forecasting activities, community colleges can answer four crucial questions: Where is the institution now? Where is it going and where will it drift without planning for the future? Where does it want to go to serve its students and the community the best it can? and What does it have to change to get where it needs and wants to go? (Morrison, Renfo, and Boucher, 1984).

Most community colleges engage in a variety of activities that provide information from the external environment for planning purposes; one example is the local advisory committee composed of employers for a specific technical program. Jain (1984) has identified four phases of evolution in organizations. His phase 1, the primitive phase, is when an institution faces an environment as it appears, with exposure to information without purpose and effort. Phase 2, the ad-hoc phase, is when the institution watches out for the likely impact of the environment on the institution; the institution is sensitive to information on specific issues, and scans only to enhance understanding of a specific event. Phase 3, the reactive phase, is when the organization deals with the environment to protect its future. Scanning is an unstructured and random effort with no specific information collected. Scanning is done in order for an institution to make appropriate responses to competition or to markets. In phase 4, the proactive phase, the organization engages in strategic scanning in order to be on the lookout for its competitive advantage. Scanning is a structured and deliberate effort to collect specific information using an established methodology for analysis. Scanning is purposeful in that the institution wishes to forecast the environment in order to design its future.

A systematic and ongoing process of external environmental scanning and forecasting enables a college to monitor selected trends, track emerging issues, and assess major events. This information helps the college define its preferred future by setting organizational goals, developing and implementing specific action steps, and monitoring the effects of these actions on the college.

Scanning for Changes

Establishing a systematic and ongoing scanning system requires effort and resources. It must have the commitment and support of the CEO. Its importance lies in its ability to bring information forward for forces shaping the region, nation, or society in general (Morrison and Held, 1989). *Trends* are often longitudinal in that they have been observed over time. Examples include the increasingly multicultural and multilingual composition of the U.S. labor force, and the growing reliance on student loans leading to more student debts.

An *event* is a discrete, confirmable occurrence that makes the future different from the past (Morrison and Held, 1989). An event is often a one-time phenomenon, usually visible or dramatic, and has a short-term effect on the system. An event focuses attention on an occurrence at one point in time. In contrast with a trend, an event can be viewed as cross-sectional. For example: the explosion of the shuttle *Challenger* and the loss of the astronauts was an event; the lack of public support for space exploration and the lack of a compelling focus and reason for the space program is a trend. College students' growing reliance on student loans as opposed to grants, and the rise in debt and delinquency by students is a trend. The passage of federal legislation to require colleges with high student default rates to institute plans to reduce these rates or face termination of participation in aid programs is an event.

An *emerging issue* is a potential controversy that arises out of a trend or event, which may require some form of response (Morrison and Held, 1989). In general, an emerging issue is often unclear and unsettled, in large measure because it involves a conflict among interest groups and revolves around clashing values. For example, in the United States there is a widening gap between those doing well and those who, despite their struggles, may never acquire the standard of living of their parents or grandparents. Referred to as "Generation X" or the "baby busters," this group is not doing as well in the marketplace as they had expected or hoped, though they may believe their status will improve as time goes on. Increasingly, their generational spokespersons are questioning the distribution of income and government assistance to those much older. This looming generational conflict and its implications for higher education awaits colleges and universities. Though dormant now, the future force of this divergence of interests illustrates what is meant by an emerging issue.

The challenge for community colleges is to identify the particular trends, events, and emerging issues that will affect them, and to use this information in shaping a preferred future, as opposed to reacting to an imposed future. Eastern Iowa Community College District (EICCD) in Davenport, Iowa, provides a useful example of how a community college utilized information obtained by monitoring a series of events, and thereby identified a trend with great impact on its organization. This district serves largely rural counties in the most eastern section of Iowa. In 1984, college staff became aware of the increasing impact of federal rules and regulations regarding the handling and disposal of hazardous materials on its local industries. Proposed state regulations and a growing public awareness regarding the need to protect the environment created the need for a variety of programs in environmental technologies. The EICCD was able to utilize this information to obtain funding from the U.S. Environmental Protection Agency to develop a nationally validated competency-based program in hazardous materials technology. The EICCD has been at the forefront of curriculum and program development across a broad spectrum of environmental programs. Working with Kirkwood Community College in Cedar Rapids, Iowa, it has formed the Hazardous Materials Training and Research Institute, a nationally recognized organization that provides technical assistance to other community colleges across the United States.

Another example of the use of external environmental scanning and forecasting is in long-range planning. Through involvement of an environmental scanning committee, Catonsville Community College (Baltimore, Maryland) identified and selected external trends in its environment most consequential to its future. The trends were examined by all function units of the college, and were used as the basis for developing goals and objectives that would move the college into its preferred future.

Another use of external environmental scanning and forecasting is in mission refinement. Recently Kalamazoo Valley Community College (Kalamazoo, Michigan) involved faculty, administrators, and support staff in scan teams to identify likely and consequential changes to the future of the many rural communities it serves in western Michigan. Scan teams identified trends in the environment. College faculty and staff selected a core of key or driving trends, and used these core trends to draft a new and future-oriented mission statement.

Scanning Sources and Scan Teams

Sources of materials involved in a scanning effort are unlimited. Some sources can be viewed as formal: professional journals, newspapers, and magazines; government reports; futurist newsletters; local, state, and federal planning reports; and reports from corporations, banks, and the nonprofit sector. Other sources are more informal: off-the-wall and visionary materials; video, electronic, and other nonprint technology; art and music; theater and performing arts presentations; and radio and TV talk shows.

Scan teams are essential, and their composition and role is critical. In the ideal case, community colleges should endorse the notion that everyone is a scanner and is welcome to join in a scan team. All members of the college community—faculty, staff, students, administrators, board, and community members—should be welcome to participate. From president to janitor, all college employees read and think about the implications of the material on them, their families, and their community. Scan teams should meet on a regular basis to share completed scan abstracts and to discuss change and its implications for the college. Scan team members should immediately bring to the attention of college leaders information and implications they believe are so critical that time cannot delay their presentation. While six to eight members constitute an ideal scan team, the composition of the team is equally important. The members of the team should be volunteers who are subject-matter experts and inquisitive in nature. These individuals should possess keen minds, be analytical, and offer opposing views and implications. They should be especially good at asking questions. Those who walk to the beat of "a different drummer" are especially helpful as members. Community representatives are often valuable as members of a team; however, they should be asked to join a team only after the college believes it has mastered scanning and feels comfortable and confident in its ability to lead this effort.

Scan information is important to report and disseminate so that it may be considered for its implications in the future of the organization. Experience suggests that a summary report with the trends and emerging issues found consequential to the college's future should be presented to the college community and especially to those involved in planning. Sustaining the scanning momentum is dependent on the tangible outcomes resulting from its use by the college. When scanning is used to refine an institution's mission and goals, improve its planning process, develop new programs, revise existing curriculum, define its budget requests and spending plans, then those who serve as scanners are more likely to believe that their participation makes a positive difference in the future of their college, and for the students and community they serve.

Supporting Scanning and Forecasting

External environmental scanning can be done on a modest budget—and more often makes do with a "shoestring" budget. Whatever the funding, scanning and forecasting requires the active and ongoing support of the CEO and other college leaders as well as institutional recognition. However, an institution does not need to establish a scanning and forecasting office complete with computers, software, and support personnel. Indeed, the concept of wide participation in the scanning process is at odds with such a notion. What is important is the dissemination and use of the information for planning purposes. Interest can be sustained and participation fostered by an ongoing program of staff development. Staff development activities should address what is environmental scanning, how to scan, and the use of scanning information to identify and prioritize those trends and events most consequential to the short and long-term interest of the institution.

Conclusion

Community colleges are often the major locus for change and development in their areas, and they can be the centerpiece for community planning and service. College efforts lead communities into planning for and responding to a future that has been identified and shaped by an active external environmental scanning and forecasting activity. External environmental scanning and forecasting will be increasingly important for community colleges that wish to shape a preferred future. While establishing, supporting, and using a scanning and forecasting capability takes preparation and development time, institutionalization of it in the fabric and membership of the college is well worth the effort. The benefits it brings will enhance the community college's effectiveness, public support, and community pride.

References

Coates, J. F. *Issues Management: How You Can Play, Organize, and Manage for the Future.* Mount Airy, Md.: Lomond, 1986.

Friedel, J. N., Coker, D. R., and Blong, J. T. "A Survey of Environmental Scanning in U.S. Technical and Community Colleges." Paper presented at the 31st annual conference of the Association for Institutional Research, San Francisco, May 26–29, 1991. (ED 333 923)

Hallett, J. J. *Worklife Visions: Redefining Work for the Information Economy.* Alexandria, Va.: American Society for Personnel Administration, 1987.

Jain, S. C. "Environmental Scanning in U.S. Corporations." *Long-Range Planning,* Apr. 1984, 17, 117–128.

Morrison, J. L. "Environmental Scanning." In M. A. Whiteley, J. D. Porter, and R. H. Fensk (eds.), *The Primer for Institutional Research.* Tallahassee, Fla.: Association for Institutional Research, 1992.

Morrison, J. L., and Held, W. G. "Developing Environmental Scanning/Forecasting Systems to Augment Community College Planning." *Journal of the Virginia Community College Association,* Spring 1989, 4, 12–20.

Morrison, J. L., Renfo, W. L., and Boucher, W. I. *Futures Research and the Strategic Planning Process: Implications for Higher Education.* Washington, D.C.: Association for the Study of Higher Education, 1984.

JANICE NAHRA FRIEDEL *is president of Lexington Community College, Lexington, Kentucky.*

JOEL D. LAPIN *is professor of sociology at Catonsville Community College in Baltimore County, Maryland.*

The rural community college needs to assume a leading role in supporting rural development, utilizing strategies that are consistent with its institutional mission and that ensure economic feasibility, quality, and excellence.

Program Development in the Rural Community College

Anne S. McNutt

To consider program development in the rural community college, one must first examine the meaning of the term *rural*. Because the label applies to such a wide variety of geographic and economic settings, no general characterization fits them all (Hobbs, 1992). However, "for the most part the nation's rural areas are older and poorer than urbanized America. And they are getting more so" (Gimlin, 1990, p. 414). According to Treadway, the rural context today is "diversifying, less agriculturally oriented, diminishing in population, aging, less educated, less technology oriented, and less well off economically than its metro-based counterpart sector" (1992, p. 138). In spite of these differences, because of public policies, transportation, and communication technology, rural areas in the United States today have largely been incorporated into mainstream society, for people living in rural areas watch the same TV programs, consume the same products, and work at many of the same jobs as their urban counterparts (Hobbs, 1992).

Education offered by the community college supports economic and community development in the United States whether in a rural or urban setting. Each community college tailors its programs to meet unique local needs and circumstances. How does the college serving vast and sparsely populated expanses—rural areas that range from resort communities to areas lying just beyond suburbs to Indian reservations to mining communities—tailor its programs? To support rural development, education should be both traditional and nontraditional, tailored to the diverse needs of the residents of the rural community. The United States today, especially rural areas, requires a more informed citizenry. This provides a special challenge to the rural community college.

NEW DIRECTIONS FOR COMMUNITY COLLEGES, no. 90, Summer 1995 © Jossey-Bass Inc., Publishers

Characteristics of the Rural College

How is the community college that serves these rural communities distinguished from its larger, more urban counterpart? Within the American Association of Community Colleges (AACC), almost six hundred institutions consider themselves to be either rural or small, or both (Vineyard, 1979, p. 29). The Task Force on Rural Community Colleges identified the rural community college as publicly supported, located in a population center of under 10,000, serving a vast geographic area, and having a programmatic thrust toward comprehensiveness. In 1979, about two-thirds of these rural colleges enrolled fewer than 1,000 students (Vineyard, 1979, p. 31). Even in 1990, according to *A Summary of Selected National Data Pertaining to Community, Technical and Junior Colleges,* 25 percent of all public community colleges were small, enrolling fewer than 1,390 students (American Association of Community and Junior Colleges, 1990, p. 5).

Supporting the Needs of the Community

As unique as the communities that they serve, these colleges offer widely varying programs. Some community colleges provide a core curriculum with a more liberal perspective in career development than do others. Program mix and program development vary from one community college to another as each college tailors its programs to meet the diverse needs of the residents of the communities it serves. Regardless of its program mix, the community college—because of its tendency to have a rather fluid program mix—is less likely than other collegiate institutions to desire to maintain the higher educational status quo.

An ever-changing curriculum differentiates the community college from other levels of education. According to Fuller, this curriculum "is the means by which student and institutional goals are accomplished. It is knowledge, packaged, delivered, and received in a myriad of ways by a variety of persons. In essence, it is the community college" (1986, p. 41). While core program offerings exist almost universally for community colleges, each community college adds to this core those courses and programs designed to meet the unique needs of the specific communities served by the college.

Program Development

Although the processes by which the community college, either urban or rural, addresses the needs of its communities do not differ vastly, unique opportunities present themselves in program development at the rural community college. Because a primary purpose of the community college is to prepare its graduates for transfer to a senior college or university, few community college curricula have been designed specifically with contemporary rural issues in mind. However, there is one notable exception; as described in Chapter Four, the Native American tribal community colleges offer Indian-controlled programs in economic development, community health, and cultural awareness. Other exceptions include vocational-technical programs designed specifically for rural businesses and industries, and continuing education programs offered at individual work sites (Treadway, 1992).

Use of Advisory Committees. In the community college, curricular ideas and proposals emanate from a multitude of sources—advisory committees, faculty, administrators, and other stakeholders—as they assess the impact of societal trends upon their college. The community college typically relies heavily on a program advisory committee for each occupational program. Composed of individuals engaged in that specific career area or profession, often as owners of small businesses, as individuals in the health professions, or as individuals employed in industry, advisory committees propose and react to curricular ideas pertaining to their area of expertise. Frequently, advisory committees suggest changes or additions to the curricula which often result in the addition of courses (Fuller, 1986). Boone's (1992) community-based programming model has implications for developing a more comprehensive approach of working with community leaders to determine programmatic needs and to serve communities more effectively.

Role of Faculty. At the community college, as in the university setting, the faculty tend to be the most active catalysts for curricular development. Because faculty are more closely identified with the academic discipline, they usually initiate the proposed curricular changes. In some cases, however, administrators at the community college may suggest curricular changes (Fuller, 1986).

Diamond's Model. If the ever-changing curriculum is indeed the community college, how does the community college develop this ever-changing curriculum? Following a specific, effective model for curriculum design has several advantages: It allows the college to identify the key factors to be considered in sequential order, and serves as a procedural guide for those involved in the project, enabling them to understand the status of the process and their role. In addition, it improves efficiency by reducing duplication of effort and by ensuring that critical questions are asked and alternative solutions are explored (Diamond, 1989).

The process of designing, implementing, and evaluating a course or curriculum is not simple. This process requires a sensitivity to the academic setting of the project; an awareness of the capabilities and interests of the students the program is designed to serve; a knowledge and appreciation of the discipline; an understanding of the resources available to the faculty involved; and an understanding of those instructional goals required of students. While the approach must contain these elements, it should also be easy to understand and use (Diamond, 1989).

Diamond's model contains "two basic phases: (1) project selection and design and (2) production, implementation, and evaluation" (1989, p. 6). Like most models for program development, this one is generally sequential, with certain steps needing to be completed before others begin.

While Diamond's model is broadly applicable for higher education, usually the community college adopts a model of its own, with some models adhering closely to Diamond's model, while others may vary widely but be even more appropriate to the community college.

At the Technical College of the Lowcountry (TCL) in Beaufort, South Carolina, an adapted version of Diamond's model is employed as the college works to support the needs of the community. TCL's project selection and design relies heavily on the use of advisory committees and on faculty leadership. For example, the college's horticulture program was developed in response to the needs of the landscaping industry in the college's four-county service area, but most specifically for the heavily and beautifully landscaped resort of Hilton Head Island.

Assessing Program Viability

Regardless of what model the college uses, it must assess program viability. As a college considers the major issue of whether it should develop and implement a program, Foran, Pucel, Fruehling, and Johnson (1992) suggest addressing a subset of questions: Is the program consistent with the institution's mission? What are the program requirements? What are the economic feasibility, potential market, and cost requirements of the program? Can the institution competitively offer this program?

Relating to the Mission. In program development, whether in a rural or in an urban setting, community college administrators normally evaluate a program's compatibility with the college's mission. The mission statement typically includes information about the level of the programs, the type of programs, the content fields, and the types of occupational or technical training provided (Foran, Pucel, Fruehling, and Johnson, 1992).

Evaluating Program Requirements. Once an institution has decided that a proposed new program appropriately falls within the curricular offerings as defined by the college's mission, the college must then determine specific program requirements. Information about available jobs—clusters, functions, skill requirements, salaries, and demand—comprises an essential part of program requirements. Both the *Dictionary of Occupational Titles* (DOT) and the *Occupational Outlook Handbook,* published by the United States Department of Labor, provide valuable information about jobs (Foran, Pucel, Fruehling, and Johnson, 1992). As the college examines program requirements, it considers potential student characteristics and typically answers a series of questions: Will this program attract students similar to those already enrolled at the college? Or will the program attract a group of students who differ substantially enough from the current student that such special support services as additional counseling or remedial education will be necessary? Will the proposed curriculum need to be offered at special times or locations? Does the proposed program have either special legal requirements or program accreditation?

Considering Economic Feasibility. After the institution examines a proposed program and determines that the program is a viable one, the college then considers whether the program is economically feasible. At this point in the program development process, special issues emerge for the rural community college. When the college collects information on the economic feasibility of the program, it examines information on the size of the potential market for the program and on the cost of offering the program. Both the employment demand for graduates and the potential student demand for the program determine the potential market for the program (Foran, Pucel, Fruehling, and Johnson, 1992). Programs at the rural community college are likely to have smaller enrollments than those at the urban college simply because of the vast difference in the population base of the communities that the college serves.

The information revolution also presents special opportunities to community colleges, for the impact of technology on curricular offerings is significant and expensive. Pierce and Bragg (1984, p. 73) noted that "the ability of any community college to mount high technology programs will depend on the local job market for the program's completers and on the availability of resources for equipment, faculty and facilities." This availability of resources poses unique challenges for the rural community college, for rural areas are less likely to have substantial numbers of high-tech jobs and are less likely to have adequate resources available for equipment, faculty, and facilities than their more urban counterparts. However, creative rural community colleges can capably meet these challenges. For example, when the electronics advisory committee at the Technical College of the Lowcountry (TCL) indicated that fiber optics should be added to the curriculum, the college aggressively and actively sought the resources needed. Because of a grant from Hargray Telephone Company, TCL students have the advantage of a state-of-the-art fiber-optics lab.

State offices of jobs and training along with DOT information prove helpful in determining demand for graduates. Administrators at the rural community college may find that while a large amount of data concerning job supply and demand exists, there may be virtually none for the specific geographic area their college serves.

Determining student demand requires skills in the assessment of student interest. Again, the rural community college faces special problems. Usually the rural college serves an area that is sparsely populated, so it may not have the necessary critical mass of students to begin a new program. Assessment of student interest is typically performed by the college. While the larger, urban college—typically with more staff—usually has at least one administrator who is responsible for either institutional research or curriculum development or both, this may not be the case at the rural college. The assessment of student interest may be left to an administrator who has no specific training or skills in either research or curriculum development.

Once the market for the program has been determined, the cost requirements of operating the program can be established to assess its economic feasibility. The college should establish any additional costs for the program by including those dollars that would be expended on additional resources for the new program. Costs to be considered include those for instructors, support personnel, classroom and laboratory space, equipment, security, remodeling, and any other expenses (Foran, Pucel, Fruehling, and Johnson, 1992).

For a new program to be cost-effective, expenditures for the program must be offset by adequate income derived from tuition, state funding, grants, endowments, special project funds, and other sources (Foran, Pucel, Fruehling, and Johnson, 1992). Here again, the rural community college may encounter more difficulties than its urban counterpart. Projected tuition revenue at a rural college attributed to a new program will usually be less than that in the larger, more urban college simply because of a smaller population base from which to attract students. Thus, beginning a new program in fiber optics will likely attract a greater enrollment in an urban area than in a rural area.

As it assesses the economic feasibility of a new program, the rural community college would be well served to consider that "an institution with limited resources and clear objectives that uses the resources effectively to achieve the objectives is far more likely to provide quality education than some of its more affluent counterparts" (Millard, 1991, p. 135).

Determining Competitive Position.   Once a college has decided that the program is cost-effective, the college should then determine its competitive position for offering the proposed program. Typically a college will analyze data gathered up to this point on competitive institutions offering the program, the costs of the program, potential income, and any unique advantages or disadvantages to the institution. While an urban institution often enjoys the advantage of offering a given program because it is located close to a major employer of graduates, the rural college enjoys this competitive advantage less frequently. Often, though, the rural institution will not have as many competitors for its programs as its more urban counterpart.

Ensuring Quality and Excellence in Programs

As a college considers developing programs, quality is of paramount importance. Astin suggests that quality and true excellence lie "in the institution's ability to have a favorable impact, to enhance the intellectual and scholarly development of the student, to make a positive difference in the student's life" (1986, p. 17). Sometimes students and communities in rural areas seem to appreciate more than their urban counterparts the difference that a college in this setting can and does make. Perhaps because of a dearth of other opportunities, the rural community college has more opportunity than its urban counterpart to make a difference, and to reflect quality and true excellence.

Millard defines quality as "the extent to which an institution or program effectively utilizes its resources to achieve its appropriate educational objectives" (1991, p. 136). Therein lie the real challenge and opportunity for the rural community college: to use its very limited resources wisely to achieve its educational objectives effectively.

Capturing New Opportunities

Although the community college today constitutes the most vibrant segment of higher education, to retain this edge community college administrators must accept new challenges in the curricular areas: providing balance between liberal arts and occupational education; developing approaches to learning and teaching that meet the needs of a diverse student population; and expanding lifelong education opportunities (Norris, 1984). As the avenue for providing this balance, developing these approaches, and expanding opportunities, program development will become even more important in the future in the community college. Administrators involved in program development would be wise to adopt a model that meets their needs.

New audiences for the community college include nontraditional students—students aged twenty-five and older returning to work on a degree, professionals required by state law to continue their education, retirees interested in the sheer joy of learning, displaced workers seeking to replace jobs lost to high-technology alternatives, special groups of immigrants and first-generation U.S. citizens seeking job skills and education, and women planning to enter the job market after their children are grown (Apps, 1988). For the rural college located in the Sunbelt, in a resort area, or in any area that promotes "quality of life," another group of students is also important—the retirees.

How does the diversity of adult learners, of traditional and nontraditional students with their multitude of needs and interests, influence a college's curriculum? Obviously, the curriculum of the rural community college will address the needs of a diverse group of students just as the curriculum of a larger, more urban college does. Business and professional people, the elderly, and career changers will also need different services from traditional students even when their curricular needs are quite similar.

Conclusion

While the opportunities for the rural community college in program development do not differ markedly from those of its more urban counterpart, the resources differ substantially. Rural areas have unfortunately come to the point of having to address many of the same issues that urban areas address, but without the resources, without the larger core of professionals, and without the necessary infrastructure. In addressing the critical programmatic needs of its communities, the rural community college should recognize that it is not the amount of resources a college has but how well those resources are used to meet the needs of the students and the community that is important.

References

American Association of Community and Junior Colleges. *A Summary of Selected National Data Pertaining to Community, Technical and Junior Colleges: Community Colleges, Where America Goes to College.* Washington, D.C.: American Association of Community and Junior Colleges, 1990.

Apps, J. W. *Higher Education in a Learning Society: Meeting New Demands for Education and Training.* San Francisco: Jossey-Bass, 1988.

Astin, A. W. "Achieving Educational Excellence." In Oklahoma Network for Continuing Higher Education, *The Expanding Knowledge Base.* Oklahoma City: Oklahoma State Regents for Higher Education, 1986.

Boone, E. J. "Community-Based Programming: An Opportunity and Imperative for the Community College." *Community College Review,* 1992, *20* (3), 8–20.

Diamond, R. M. *Designing and Improving Courses and Curricula in Higher Education: A Systematic Approach.* San Francisco: Jossey-Bass, 1989.

Foran, J. V., Pucel, D. V., Fruehling, R. T., and Johnson, J. C. *Effective Curriculum Planning: Performances, Standards and Outcomes.* Eden Prairie, Minn.: Paradigm, 1992.

Fuller, J. W. *Community College Curricula: Circa 1990. An Anthology.* Galesburg, Ill.: Blick, 1986.

Gimlin, H. "The Continuing Decline of Rural America." *Editorial Research Reports.* Washington, D.C.: Congressional Quarterly, July 20, 1990.

Hobbs, D. "The Rural Context for Education: Adjusting the Images." In M. W. Galbraith (ed.), *Education in the Rural American Community: A Lifelong Process.* Malabar, Fla.: Krieger, 1992.

Millard, R. M. *Today's Myths and Tomorrow's Realities: Overcoming Obstacles to Academic Leadership in the Twenty-First Century.* San Francisco: Jossey-Bass, 1991.

Norris, N. A. "The Community College as a Future-Oriented Community Learning System." In R. J. Brass (ed.), *Community Colleges, the Future, and SPOD: Staff, Program, and Organizational Development.* Stillwater, Okla.: New Forums Press, 1984.

Pierce, D. R., and Bragg, A. K. "The Community College Challenge for the Future: A State Agency Viewpoint." In R. J. Brass (ed.), *Community Colleges, the Future, and SPOD: Staff, Program, and Organizational Development.* Stillwater, Okla.: New Forums Press, 1984.

Treadway, D. M. "Higher Education." In M. W. Galbraith (ed.), *Education in the Rural American Community: A Lifelong Process.* Malabar, Fla.: Krieger, 1992.

Vineyard, E. E. "American Association of Community and Junior Colleges Task Force Report: The Rural Community College." *Community College Review,* 1979, 6 (3), 29–45.

ANNE S. MCNUTT is president of Technical College of the Lowcountry, Beaufort, South Carolina.

*Using a community-based model, the rural community college can
bring leaders from education, government, and the private sector to
focus on strategies that maximize existing resources through careful
leveraging and cooperative communication.*

Civic Trusteeship: A Collaborative Model for Community Development

Millicent M. Valek

It is not surprising that the interpretation of the community college mission is
in a constant state of transition, with extensive discussion about where U.S.
higher education may wind up as a result. However, the elasticity of the mission is inevitable; community colleges have always had a symbiotic relationship
with their local communities. That is, they reflect the unique characteristics of
the communities they serve and are influenced by the struggles of their local
constituency. In fact, it is the broad nature of the mission with its community-
based characteristics that distinguishes the community college within U.S.
higher education. It provides flexibility and calls for creative leadership to deal
with pressing needs and complex social issues as well as traditional academic
programming.

Community colleges are major players in rural settings. They assist community agencies and governments in developing their capacity for functioning
within the system in which they find themselves through partnerships that
allow participants to plan effectively for and capitalize on impending change.
Academia serves as the resource for cutting-edge information regarding national
issues, emerging technologies, and new ideas. Any discussion of the mission of
community colleges must consider the context of the major transformation now
occurring in our society, and must also address the rural college's role in capacity building that provides for insightful action in periods of change.

Community and College Interdependence

Despite concern that the community college mission is already critically
overextended, a growing number of colleges are committed to helping

communities meet their most pressing needs, needs that cannot be adequately addressed through academic programming alone. Leaders within these colleges recognize that the college and the community are interdependent. For years, leaders within the community college field have noted that what is needed is a goal that includes not just responsiveness to needs but leadership in the improvement of all aspects of community life. Beyond being community based, colleges must aim at human and community renewal.

Roueche and Johnson (1994) point out that for 350 years U.S. higher education has continued to broaden its mission and to evolve in response to the needs of its society. With the challenges facing today's citizenry, it is absolutely essential that the community college assume its full role of community development and renewal. This does not mean an abandonment of the traditional mission but rather a full realization of the mission that recognizes the college's growing interdependency with its community and the expectation of involvement as a full partner in resolving pressing issues—whatever they may be.

Capacity Building. Communities across the nation are struggling with myriad concerns, including unemployment, underemployment, breakdown of family units, overburdened education systems, increases in crime and violence, and drastic changes in the way of life as they have always known it. Compounding these problems, the avenues available for addressing issues are often so disjointed and segmented that numerous agencies may spend scarce resources on independent attempts to solve one problem while other—and equally troubling—problems remain unaddressed by any of them. This fragmented approach is frustrating at best, and in most cases, it is dysfunctional. Too often public debate polarizes support so much that even when decisions are reached, the solutions fail.

An often overlooked foundation that is necessary for the health of a community is that of capacity building. This covers activities that assist community organizations in developing the capacity to participate effectively in community and economic development. It results in the building of partnerships, enhanced community support, and the establishment of forums for creating greater potential for participation by a spectrum of community agencies and institutions. Capacity building thus becomes the backbone for comprehensive development efforts that involve multiple parties and require effective communication networks for successful implementation.

Rural Colleges and Capacity Building. Economic diversification is a major goal of development activities, especially in rural areas dependent on a single or a few major industries. Diversification leads to economic growth, less unemployment, and a wider range of opportunities for a broader spectrum of people. It also puts a community in a position where it is much less vulnerable to economic shifts and trends.

When reviewing the literature on economic development, patterns emerge that serve as keys to successful rural initiatives. Thomas (1988) finds that hallmarks of successful efforts include capitalizing on existing resources. These include human, natural, and economic resources. Emerging strategies incorporate education into their long-term efforts. This goes beyond viewing educational institutions as the providers of specialty training programs. Instead, communities turn to educational institutions as partners in the facilitation of economic development activities that call for collaboration and the breakdown of traditional political divisions.

Another key to successful initiatives is long-term consistency. Communities that incorporate strong planning components in their programs or goals and emphasize research for planning as the starting point have a track record for producing positive outcomes. They are able to provide long-term consistency, building solid foundations for continued progress fifteen to twenty years into the future.

The management of transition becomes a critical consideration when an economic base is on the verge of diversification. More often than not, transition occurs due to external forces such as a changing world economy, advances in technology, or national policies. While there may have been little local control over the driving forces of change, there is considerable local impact. In situations like these, the critical issue becomes the capacity of the local community to manage change rather than simply react to change imposed from outside. Banach and Lorenzo (1993) note that the uncertainty that characterizes today's business environment creates uneasiness. It really leaves only two basic choices: function with respect to the system or be in jeopardy.

Civic Trusteeship Model

Although their solution is still evolving, the Yuma County (Arizona) experience may be useful to other communities facing imminent change and explosive growth. This model brings the community's stakeholders together to discuss common social and economic issues and provides the basis for the development of collaborative resolutions to community problems. In order to understand the significance of the Yuma County Civic Trusteeship concept, however, it is important to be aware of community demographics and the driving forces that emphasized the urgency for a community development forum of this magnitude.

Community Demographics. Yuma County is located in southwest Arizona, contiguous to the Mexico and California borders. Its geographic location in the corner of the state fosters a feeling of isolation—reasonably enough, with the nearest metropolitan area at least a three-hour drive away. According to 1990 Census data, 106,895 people live in Yuma County. Unemployment rates for 1992 ranged from a high of 30.1 percent in July to a low of 14.6 percent in February. The county's longtime growth rate has averaged a steady increase of 4 percent per year.

Driving Forces. After a lengthy history of slow, steady growth, Yuma County leaders realized that there were a number of internal and external factors indicating that the growth rate might quickly become 10 to 15 percent annually. These included the impending passage of the North American Free

Trade Agreement; several large industrial employers considering relocation to Yuma; over 500,000 square feet of additional retail space in final planning stages; an available Municipal and Industrial water supply attractive to prospective industries; close proximity to Southern California, Mexico, and Arizona markets; potential increases in military base loading due to Department of Defense restructuring; and an 8,500-acre new mixed-use development project estimated to provide 85,000 new jobs with an estimated population of 250,000 sited for a community just across the border in San Luis Rio Colorado, Sonora, Mexico.

Development of the Model. Community leaders recognized that, regardless of whether or not all of these factors became reality, change was imminent and that measures were needed to support year-round employment. The community was facing explosive growth and there was need for a coordinated and cooperative response. Late in 1992, leaders and decision makers representing some forty agencies, organizations, and municipalities came together to discuss potential impacts on their individual agencies and on the community as a whole.

Early steps included the identification of who should be involved and meetings with these leaders to discuss the importance of working together to build a forum for participation and action. A basis for getting this group off the ground and functioning was the provision of structural lines for the organization with roles and expectations outlined. Room for flexibility and ownership by those pioneering the organization was accommodated through this loosely structured start. All participating organizations were invited to submit nominations for the eleven-member Board of Directors serving as the steering committee for the project. While board membership must be at the CEO or chair level, working groups addressing specific issues have a much broader base of participation and input. Initially, three working groups were identified. One was charged with developing a mission statement for the Civic Trusteeship, another to develop plans for financing the management of the program and selected cooperative efforts that emerged as the a result of ongoing discussions, and a third group to identify specific issues within the community that needed to be addressed.

Issues Task Force. The most active group working under the auspices of the Civic Trusteeship is the Issues Task Force. Its charge, early on, was to identify the most pressing issues that required response from this organization. Clearly assessing community needs, this group began to determine specifications for the development of a data base for community planning. A working group of volunteers representing thirteen different organizations met over a period of six weeks to develop the specifications for an impact analysis study and modeling program to assess alternative growth scenarios. Private funding along with membership contributions provide the monetary basis for the award of this bid for services. Discussion is under way regarding data storage and systems to allow equal access to members, ensure that data are regularly updated, and provide computer modeling capabilities. Resources already available, such as information in the City and County Geographical Information Systems, will be shared through the Civic Trusteeship with other parties interested in this kind of planning and management data.

Outcomes. A number of specific outcomes have already been realized through the Yuma County Civic Trusteeship. These include significant private sector investments to provide for the hiring of a project coordinator and the establishment of a Civic Trusteeship office. A series of town meetings and early discussions led to coordinated industrial recruitment efforts and external federal funding applications. In addition, city and county governments began working closely together to open negotiations with the water district in order to provide for anticipated needs through the next decade. Overall, increased communication on a regular basis has led, and will continue to lead, to more effective and efficient planning for future community development.

Of equal importance is the less tangible but highly enviable community climate that supports collaboration between the school districts, college, university, city and county governments, and the private sector for not only responding to change but also for planning. Regardless of personal conflicts regarding "growth" versus "no growth" values, there is a common realization that a change in size necessitates a change in structure if the community is to continue functioning. Wilson (1977) noted almost two decades ago that management of scale continues to be one of the major difficulties besetting modern society. Wilson's perspective on growth continues to be accurate today, for reasons that are largely political. Bringing together local agencies, governments, educational districts, water districts, police departments, and so on, each with their sovereignties, is no easy task. Faced with greater demands, escalating costs, and shrinking resources, the natural organizational instinct is to focus on protecting boundaries and internal constituencies. United action is not an attribute with which communities are inherently endowed. The promise of the Civic Trusteeship is that it continues to serve as the catalyzing agent consolidating and directing energies in a positive way. At the very least, it provides the simple recognition that effective functioning for a community in transition means that no single group can ever wholly have its own way. What is called for is better communication, the ability to plan together, and the desire to leverage scarce resources to serve the general good.

Conclusion

The community college's role in this type of collaborative effort is of particular consequence due to its very nature. The college is viewed as neutral turf, an entity devoid of highly political connections. It is on these grounds that community members are willing to openly share information, to debate in a collegial fashion, and to plan for the good of the whole. Precautions must be taken by the community college to always remain in the role of facilitator— not power broker. It is the essential foundation for being able to successfully build this type of model.

Even so, no higher education system can serve as a panacea for community development. There are a multiplicity of factors that come into play that affect the vitality and health of a region. However, it is clearly within the mission of the community college to assume an active role in contributing to the development of a community and its capacity to sustain long-term economic and quality of life goals. Building partnerships that stimulate and abet insightful decision making is critical to effective functioning in a changing world.

References

Banach, W. J., and Lorenzo, A. L. *Toward a New Model for Thinking and Planning: The Emerging Context of Life in America*. Warren, Mich.: Macomb Press, 1993.

Roueche, J. E., and Johnson, L. "A New View of American Higher Education." *Leadership Abstracts*, 1994, 7 (1).

Thomas, M. *Profiles in Rural Economic Development: A Guidebook of Selected Successful Rural Area Initiatives*. Washington, D.C.: Economic Development Administration, 1988.

Wilson, K. D. (ed.). *Prospects for Growth: Changing Expectations for the Future*. New York: Praeger, 1977.

MILLICENT M. VALEK *is vice president for academic affairs at Arizona Western College, Yuma.*

There has been little research about what motivates adults to enroll in rural community college distance education programs. One case study was conducted in Maine to examine these motivations and their implications for rural community colleges; its findings are examined here.

Rural Adults in Community College Distance Education: What Motivates Them to Enroll?

Pamela S. MacBrayne

Economic and social changes have increased the number of rural adults desiring access to college programs. Although many colleges are attempting to serve these students, a review of the literature indicates that little research has been conducted to ascertain what motivates rural adults to enroll in postsecondary distance education. This information holds particular importance for rural community colleges, as their distance education programs must serve diverse populations of students throughout large geographic areas. Without understanding student motivations, it is difficult for educators to design programs and services to meet the educational needs and aspirations of these students and encourage their academic success.

In an effort to obtain an understanding of motivation to enroll, the author conducted a study of rural adults enrolled in a distance education program in Maine. In 1985, despite the existence of seven university and six technical college campuses, only one-third of the state's population lived within a twenty-five-mile commute of a public postsecondary institution (Connick and MacBrayne, 1988). In an effort to provide greater access to education, the University of Maine at Augusta proposed the development of the Community College of Maine (renamed the Education Network of Maine), a distance education program designed to serve as a statewide community college system for rural residents by means of new and existing off-campus centers, a new interactive television system, and other electronic technologies. Inaugurated in September 1989, its goal was to provide students in the off-campus locations with academic instruction and student support services comparable to those received by students in the on-campus studio classroom.

The study examined the motivations of rural adult learners to enroll in an associate degree distance education program. Specifically, it addressed three related research questions: Who enrolled and what reasons did they give for doing so? What underlying motivations influenced the decision to enroll in college? What barriers and facilitators affected the enrollment decision?

A questionnaire was completed by 672 students enrolled in associate degree courses of the Community College of Maine's distance education program in the fall of 1989. An examination of demographics and enrollment reasons served to answer the first research question. A factor analysis provided information regarding the ways in which students responded similarly to the various reasons for enrollment. Further data analysis examined similarities and differences in the demographic characteristics of students who were highly motivated by a particular variable.

The second and third research questions explored the motivations underlying these reasons as well as the barriers and facilitators influencing the decisions to enroll. The factor analysis of the questionnaire data identified four factors that were characterized as motivational traits and one factor that was characterized as a facilitator. Interviews with thirty students provided a more in-depth examination of the students' lives as well as a deeper understanding of their primary goals and their underlying motivations to enroll in college.

Summary of Findings

Approximately three-quarters of the 672 students who responded to the questionnaire were women, and the majority were between the ages of twenty-three and forty. Almost half had previously enrolled in college courses but had not obtained degrees at the time they completed the questionnaire. Almost one-third had completed high school and were enrolled in their first college course, while almost one-fifth had already completed college degrees. Although the students lived, on average, 31.7 miles from the nearest campus, the distance education program enabled them to commute only 9.4 miles, on average, to attend their college courses.

The questionnaire asked respondents to rate thirteen reasons for enrolling in their current courses. Most students cited several reasons. The two reasons in the questionnaire to which students assigned the highest mean scores were those related to the location of the course and their interest in the course content. These were followed by the desire to obtain a degree and the importance of the course for a future career.

A factor analysis of the thirteen reasons revealed four distinct factors that were characterized as motivational traits. In order of importance to the sample, they were described as: degree seeking, information seeking, participating, and job enhancing. The fifth factor, to which the sample assigned the highest mean score, seemed to characterize a facilitator for enrollment rather than a motivational trait. It was the convenient location of the college course that was reported as the most important factor in the enrollment decision.

A review of the demographic characteristics of those scoring high in each of the five factors indicated that there were more similarities than differences. Women were somewhat overrepresented in the degree seeking, information seeking, participating and course location factors. Proportionately, more men scored high on the job enhancing trait, and they were overrepresented in the group that scored low on the four motivational traits. Regarding age, for those not highly motivated by the first four factors, the mode was eighteen to twenty-two years, while the mode for all other factors was thirty-one to forty years. The mode for educational level for all groups was "some college," with the exception of those scoring high on the participating trait. Somewhat less educated, the mode for them was "high school diploma."

Interviews with thirty students provided a means to explore their primary goals for enrolling in college as compared to reasons for choosing a particular course. Interviews were also a means to determine how, if at all, the four motivational traits were distinguishable from one another. The interviews revealed that all thirty of these rural adults cited one of three primary goals: the desire for a better future job, the desire to enhance a current job, or the desire for self-improvement. Twenty-two of these students indicated that both job-improvement and self-improvement were important to them. For some students, these goals were more focused on personal advancement while for others the driving force was more altruistic. Interviews reinforced the four motivational traits identified in the factor analysis. For those scoring high on the degree seeking trait, the completion of the degree itself did indeed appear particularly compelling. Ultimately hoping to obtain more satisfying or more lucrative jobs and seeking personal gratification, these students were stimulated to enroll by both the extrinsic and intrinsic value of the degree. These students attributed higher value to the college credential than did most others.

Information seeking was seen as the means to new knowledge that would lead to a more satisfactory future. Learning itself was considered an exciting endeavor, whether driven by an interest in the course content or by the perceived utility of the information. Although interested in completing a college degree, these students seemed to value the knowledge more than the credential.

Participating in college was important as a source of personal fulfillment for some, whether they were demonstrating the capacity to succeed in college or seeking social interaction. Enrollment in college was, for these students, a vital aspect of the process of self-discovery and autonomy. Participation was viewed as an enjoyable activity as well as a means to attain their goals.

Finally, job enhancing was important to those who enjoyed their current jobs. For some, the support and encouragement of their employers underscored the value of college coursework. For others, the college courses were mandatory. These students enrolled in college to ensure continued success in their careers.

Interviews were also conducted with students whose responses to the questionnaire indicated that none of the four motivational factors was important in their decision to enroll in that particular college course. While they were clearly motivated by several of the same motivational traits as the others interviewed, these students seemed less clear about their goals yet more desperate in their efforts to move ahead. Some were seeking a degree and others were gaining specific knowledge, but most were participating in college as a means to clarify their goals. For these students, neither the degree, the information, nor the process of participation seemed important as ends, but were viewed as a means to a better future.

Interviews also revealed the barriers that had deterred students from enrolling in college previously. Lack of time and lack of money were the most frequently cited barriers, followed by concerns about poor academic preparation, distance required to travel to college courses, and family responsibilities.

Although course location was the only facilitator included in the questionnaire, interviews showed that it was the most significant facilitator in the students' abilities to enroll in college, allowing them to overcome several barriers. Having the course located near the places they lived and worked reduced both the time and expense of commuting, as well as the expense of child care for those with young children. It also allowed more time for study, work, and family.

For some students, college campuses were a psychological barrier. Lacking the self-confidence to enroll at a campus, they cited the location of the course in a familiar community facility as an important element in the decision to enroll. Enrolling with a majority of adult students of similar age was also perceived as beneficial by many students.

Half of these rural adult students indicated the importance of the support they received from others in facilitating enrollment. Family, friends, social workers, and co-workers offered significant information and encouragement. For a portion of these students, the encouragement came from employers. Enrollment for some students was facilitated by changes in life circumstances or development changes throughout the life span. Some made the decision to enroll due to a crisis such as disability or divorce, while others took the opportunity that arose when it was no longer necessary to spend so much time with children. Having college courses available where and when they needed them was instrumental in the ability to enroll.

It appears that the importance of course location was independently related to all the motivational factors. The interviews disclosed the centrality of this factor; no matter what their primary goals or their underlying motivations, most students would not have enrolled in college if the courses had not been conveniently available.

Discussion

By the year 2000, it is likely that only one-half of the students enrolled in higher education will fit the traditional profile of the eighteen to twenty-two-year-old recent high school graduate that most postsecondary institutions were designed to serve. Given the increase in the number of adult students who are likely to enroll in distance education programs of colleges and universities, several key findings emerged from this study that will help educators meet the needs and aspirations of that significant portion of the student body. These findings will be particularly useful to educators wishing to serve rural adults.

First, the motivations of these rural adults to enroll in college are varied and complex. Like the adult learners in the studies reviewed by Merriam and Caffarella (1991) and those examined by Darkenwald and Merriam (1982), these rural adults articulated multiple and diverse reasons for enrolling. When asked the most important reason, half of the students in this study cited job-related reasons while the other half cited self-improvement. While it is often difficult to ascertain where the desire for a better job and self-improvement diverge, the reporting of self-improvement as the most important reason by 50 percent of the students was unanticipated, given the results of the triennial surveys conducted by the National Center for Education Statistics between 1969 and 1984. Of the 1984 survey participants, 64 percent cited job-related reasons as the most important for college enrollment (Merriam and Caffarella, 1991). This suggests the educators should be cognizant of both the personal and career goals of their students.

Second, this research showed that educators should not make assumptions about students' enrollment motivations based entirely on their stated goals. During the interviews, the students initially articulated similar primary goals. Upon investigation in the interviews, however, it became clear that these goals were at the surface of their thinking. Their comments illustrated a range of different underlying motivations. Listening to the students' comments revealed that the factor analysis of the questionnaire data had tapped into important underlying motivational factors.

Without knowledge of the various underlying motivations, it is not possible to comprehend the full meaning of students' decisions to enroll in college as a step toward achieving their goals. The motivational traits of degree seeking, information seeking, participating, and job enhancing brought these students to college for diverse reasons. It is these various underlying motivations that differentiate students who, on the surface, appear to enroll for similar reasons. Darkenwald and Merriam (1982) contend that because adults' motivations are typically multiple and often not obvious, educators must be sensitive to these less obvious components of motivation. This study confirms the contention that adults' motivations are multiple and diverse and suggests that educators must probe beyond the stated primary goals to obtain a complete picture of the forces that drive students to enroll.

Third, this study illustrated the value of interpreting students' primary goals and underlying motivations within the context of their life circumstances. Without understanding students' backgrounds, previous educational experiences, life transitions, level of self-confidence, perceptions of academic capabilities, fears, and aspirations, it is difficult to identify the learning activities and student support services that are crucial to success.

Fourth, this study showed that the rural adult students in the sample were older and proportionately more were female than the student population in the United States. Whether this difference is a consequence of the rural setting or the geographical and psychological accessibility of the program, it indicates that those involved with rural distance education programs should focus particular attention on the needs and aspirations of women between the ages of twenty-three and forty.

Fifth, the study disclosed that several situational barriers, especially lack of time and lack of money, and the difficulty of long-distance travel to a college campus, had precluded earlier enrollment in college. Psychological or dispositional barriers, such as the perception of poor academic preparation, the effect of earlier discouragement, and the fear of impersonal college campuses, had deterred others from enrolling sooner. While some of these rural adults had always wanted to enroll in college, others had not been motivated to do so at an earlier stage of life. Nevertheless, they cited common barriers to previous enrollment.

Finally, and perhaps most significantly, this study revealed that rural adults will enroll in college programs if courses and services are geographically and psychologically accessible at the moment at which the potential students are developmentally and situationally ready. Geographic accessibility meant reducing the time required to commute and expanding the time available for study, family, and work. It reduced the expense of transportation and child care as well as the concern about driving on secondary roads—often snowy—at night. Psychological accessibility entailed small, familiar settings with other adult students who had also been away from formal schooling for a while.

The rural students in this study, three-quarters of whom were women, required access when the timing was right for them. Developmental accessibility meant the availability of college courses at the appropriate stage of life. For some, the desire to enroll in college had been building for years, but time, money, and family responsibilities had prevented them from enrolling. When these circumstances changed, their eclipsed dreams and continued thirst for better jobs and self-improvement propelled them toward college. For others, a sudden disability or crisis provided the impetus to begin or reenter college. Their quests were often precipitated by age, shifting family responsibilities, physical limitations, or job requirements. A confluence of events in their lives, coupled with the support of others and the availability of college programs, often triggered enrollment in college as the means to achieve life and career goals.

The data from this study confirm the accuracy of Cross's (1981) Chain of Response model, in which she contends that participation in a learning activity is the result not of a single act but of a chain of responses based on an evaluation of the individual's position in his or her environment. For most of these rural adult students, it would not have been possible to pursue their goals or act upon their underlying motivations had college courses not been conveniently available, despite the strength of their aspirations. Although the convenient location of the course does not appear to be a motivation, it does facilitate enrollment when the motivation already exists. The students interviewed for this study did not enroll just because the courses were available locally; they wanted better futures for themselves. Having the courses locally available allowed them to pursue their goals.

Implications

This study has substantial implications for those involved in higher education, particularly for rural community colleges. Educators should be sensitive to the importance of both the geographic and psychological accessibility necessary for adults to overcome previous barriers, pursue their goals, and fulfill their underlying motivations. The location of courses close to home reduces the need to travel over rural roads and helps to mitigate the barriers of time and expense related to commuting. Without convenient locations and helpful, supportive staff, many adults will be too intimidated to enroll.

Educators who understand the varied backgrounds, life circumstances, and developmental stages of adult learners can help facilitate their enrollment in college when it is needed. As Garrison (1989) suggests, the technologies exist today to allow learners to study when and where they choose and to have all the guidance and support they require or request. The results of this study imply that it is the responsibility of educators to harness these technologies, adapt the teaching process, and provide appropriate support services to accommodate these learners.

Adults need access to relevant educational programs and support services. The data from this study indicate that many rural adults, like adults in previous studies, are enrolled for job-related reasons. Access to career information and academic advising is a hallmark of community colleges. Students desiring new jobs find it particularly helpful to examine what aspects of current or past jobs they did and did not like in an effort to focus on future careers. Assisting students to target specific careers allows them to tailor their academic programs appropriately. Internships, job-shadowing, and other work-experience programs assist them in developing job skills within the contexts of their degrees. And workshops in résumé writing and interviewing skills help them obtain their goals.

This study confirmed Cross's (1981) contention that more women than men would pursue education to prepare for new jobs while more men would seek advancement in their present jobs. Nevertheless, in rural states—where many of the jobs historically held by men are disappearing with the shift from manufacturing and agricultural jobs to a service-based economy—community colleges would be wise to provide job training and career assistance to both men and women.

For students interested in self-improvement, more opportunities should be provided for assessing life experiences and participating in personal development workshops. Interest inventories, learning style assessments, personality type indicators, assertiveness training, and communication workshops would be worthwhile program components.

A process should be established that allows students to develop and articulate their personal and career goals, and support should be made available to help them achieve these goals. Because their reasons for enrolling are multiple and their underlying motivations are not always the same as their stated reasons, counselors and student advisors must probe beyond students' stated goals to ascertain underlying motivations if they are to adequately assist students in achieving their aspirations.

This study demonstrated that students not only enroll for diverse reasons, they come to college with a range of educational backgrounds. It is essential to respond to this diversity with various types of educational programs. Furthermore, once the needs and interests of adults are tapped, educators can anticipate that the demand for further education will increase and the students' interests will continue to expand. Distance education is a cost-effective way to provide the range of curricula necessary to meet the diverse needs of a geographically dispersed rural population.

This study also suggests that the focus should be not only on what is offered but also on how it is provided. Some students are motivated by the degree, some by the content of the courses, and some by the process of participating in college. Because some students enroll for neither content nor credit, more thought should be given to ways in which the range of learning needs can be addressed. A variety of offerings, including interdisciplinary courses in which the focus is on process of learning rather than specific content, would be of interest to some students.

Finally, there are many implications for further research. Another study might explore how previous education, support or discouragement, age, and other variables impact the development or hindrance of goals and motivations. Further research on the meaning of the various motivational traits identified in this study would assist community college educators in the design of programs and support services. A deeper understanding of degree seeking, information seeking, participating, and job enhancing would allow for clearer guidance and support of rural adult students. It would also be useful to obtain a better understanding of the goal of self-improvement. In this study various aspects of self-improvement were cited but the range of meanings of the goal was not pursued.

While this study examined the barriers to previous enrollment for current students, community college personnel should seek to learn more about those who have graduated from high school but have never pursued higher education. The barriers cited by the students in this study may apply, but perhaps there are others as well.

Community colleges would benefit from a greater understanding of the impact that participation in higher education has on rural adults. What is the impact on their self-esteem and self-confidence, and how does that affect their lives? It would also be helpful to examine the "addictive" nature of higher education. Some research indicates that success in educational endeavors engenders further participation; this, too, would be useful to explore.

Conclusion

Community colleges have historically developed close relationships with their students. At this time of growing student diversity and rapid development of technologies to connect students at a distance, the ability to better understand and respond to students' needs is crucial. Rural community colleges must make their programs both geographically accessible and convenient with regard to time. Technological advances have made it possible to teach students who cannot or will not attend courses on campus. These same technologies allow faculty to communicate with students in a variety of ways, including asynchronously via computer. This reduces the need to be in the same place at the same time to carry out the learning process.

Advances in technology also facilitate the individualization of instruction, allowing faculty to accommodate a variety of learning styles. Information technologies can also connect students to the resources they need to pursue personal and career goals. Given their commitment to serve a wide diversity of students, rural community colleges are well positioned to embrace distance education. The increased availability of telecommunications and technologies provides them with the tools to deliver a wide range of academic programs and the support services necessary to meet the needs of their students.

References

Connick, G., and MacBrayne, P. *Telecommunications and Educational Access.* Combined Proceedings, Sixth Annual Conference on Interactive Instruction Delivery and Third Annual Conference on Learning Technology in the Health Care Sciences, Society for Applied Learning Technology, Orlando, Fla., Feb. 24–26, 1988.

Cross, K. P. *Adults as Learners: Increasing Participation and Facilitating Learning.* San Francisco: Jossey-Bass, 1981.

Darkenwald, G., and Merriam, S. *Adult Education: Foundations of Practice.* New York: HarperCollins, 1982.

Garrison, D. R. "Distance Education." In S. Merriam and P. Cunningham (eds.), *Handbook of Adult and Continuing Education.* San Francisco: Jossey-Bass, 1989.

Merriam, S., and Caffarella, R. *Learning in Adulthood: A Comprehensive Guide.* San Francisco: Jossey-Bass, 1991.

PAMELA S. MACBRAYNE is dean of telecommunications and academic development, University of Maine System, Augusta.

This annotated bibliography focuses on rural community colleges. It lists publications on student programs, community programs, access to education, and tribal colleges.

Sources and Information:
Rural Community Colleges

Elizabeth Foote

Rural community colleges provide college transfer, workforce training, and community service to populations that otherwise would have no access to these services. They are a center of educational activity and economic development in their communities and a primary catalyst for improving the quality of rural life.

The following publications reflect the current ERIC literature on rural community colleges. Most ERIC documents (publications with ED numbers) can be viewed on microfiche at approximately nine hundred libraries worldwide. In addition, most may be ordered on microfiche or on paper from the ERIC Document Reproduction Service at (800) 443-ERIC. Journal articles are not available from this service, but may be acquired through regular library channels or purchased from the UMI Articles Clearinghouse at (800) 521-0600, extension 533.

Student Programs

Students of rural community colleges have diverse educational needs. To help meet these needs, colleges have developed a wide range of programs, including vocational education, transfer programs, high school enrichment, and personal development.

American Association of Community and Junior Colleges, Small/Rural Community Colleges Commission. *American Association of Community and Junior Colleges Small/Rural Community Colleges Commission: Exemplary Programs and Services, 1991.*

Washington, D.C.: American Association of Community and Junior Colleges, 1991. 124 pp. (ED 341 441)

Compiled by the Small/Rural Community Colleges Commission of the American Association of Community and Junior Colleges, this collection of one-page program descriptions provides information on 121 exemplary programs and services at rural two-year institutions nationwide. Each program description provides the following information: program or service title, target population, college name, executive officer, contact person, college address, telephone number, program or service narrative (up to 250 words), associated costs, personnel requirements, and key concepts for success. The program areas represented include (1) academic programs (such as the Early Admission program at Fulton-Montgomery Community College in New York, which allows qualified high school seniors to take advanced classes at the college); (2) articulation efforts (such as the 2+2 Tech Prep Articulation program at North Idaho College, which coordinates technical programs with secondary school districts); (3) developmental programs (such as the Individual College Education program at Iowa Central Community College for handicapped and learning disabled students); (4) retraining activities (such as the Gunsmithing program at Yavapai College in Arizona, which is geared toward older students who are forced to find new careers); (5) vocational programs (such as the Hardware Store Management program at Navarro College in Texas, which tries to meet a demand for better trained specialists in the hardware industry); (6) personal development programs (such as the Geritol Frolics at Brainerd Community College in Minnesota, which involves about 100 senior citizens in a professional-quality variety show); and (7) high school equivalency programs (such as the Second Chance Scholarship program at Northeastern Junior College in Colorado for disadvantaged General Equivalency Diploma graduates).

Andrews, M. B., and Hall, D. E. *Arctic College/Athabasca University Transfer Program: A Review. A Study Conducted on Behalf of Arctic College.* Edmonton, Canada: Department of Educational Administration, Alberta University, 1991. 74 pp. (ED 348 080)

In fall 1988, Arctic College (AC), Northwest Territories, Canada, in collaboration with Athabasca University (AU), Alberta, Canada, initiated the University Transfer Program (UTP) to provide first-year university education for full- and part-time students at the Yellowknife campus of AC. Program content, standards, and instruction were maintained by AU, while AC provided facilities and tutorial and administrative support. Program delivery employed both seminar instruction and home study using AU learning packages. In February 1991, a review was conducted of the UTP, examining program design, delivery methods, administration, and student satisfaction. Interviews were conducted with nine students, five instructors, four steering committee members, the director of special services at AU, and the president and vice president of Yellowknife. In addition, surveys were sent to 275 students active in UTP and 271 high school seniors. Study findings, based on a 20 percent response rate from UTP students ($N = 54$) and a 32.8 percent response rate from high school seniors ($N = 89$), included the following: (1) 83 percent of the UTP students rated the overall program quality and effectiveness as "good" or "excellent"; (2) only 8 of the 89 high school respondents indicated an interest in UTP; (3) UTP students reported administrative difficulties with registration and withdrawal procedures; and (4) UTP students participating in seminar instruction had significantly higher success rates than those involved in home study. Among the detailed recommendations provided are that instructors should receive professional development and that an explicit rationale for the goals of the UTP must be established. A review of the literature on two-year college transfer and tabulated survey responses are included.

Carlson, D. R., and Fleming, D. "Outcomes Program in a Small, Rural Community College." Paper presented at the 16th National Conference on Successful College Teaching and Administration, Orlando, Fla., Mar. 1–4, 1992. 51 pp. (ED 343 627)

Student educational outcomes and the quality of instruction are now being monitored by several programs at Worthington Community College (WCC) in southwest Minnesota. WCC, one of the twenty community colleges in the Minnesota Community College system, currently serves 875 students and has been intensifying its efforts to serve the whole service area community. An increased emphasis on outcomes by federal, state, and accrediting agencies has required WCC, and the entire state system, to streamline the handling of data to provide the outcomes information. WCC has developed and is in the process of developing systems for monitoring outcomes in the following areas: (1) assessment of incoming students in the areas of reading, writing, and mathematics, using Educational Testing Service placement tests; (2) developmental education, including the effectiveness of WCC's Academic Achievement Center, which coordinates the tutoring program and provides leadership in producing developmental courses in mathematics, reading, and writing; (3) graduate outcomes, which are measured using a survey of students one year after graduation to gather information on employment and transfer; (4) state and federal reporting, including reports on athletes and crime that must be tabulated by hand; (5) faculty evaluation; and (6) staff development. Appendixes include forms related to student assessment, vocational placement, graduation follow-up, educational participation of athletes, student evaluations of faculty in the classroom and on cable television, classroom observation, and faculty self-assessment.

Evaluation and Training Institute. *Rural Programs: Vocational Education Resource Package.* Los Angeles: Evaluation and Training Institute, 1993. 25 pp. (ED 357 790)

Designed to assist community college administrators and faculty in enhancing vocational education programs and services, this resource package on rural college programs contains information about successful program strategies and ideas currently in use in vocational education programs at rural schools within the California Community Colleges (CCC). The opening section of the report reviews institutional characteristics and administrative considerations unique to rural colleges and lists advantages of the rural college setting frequently cited in student recruitment efforts. This section also describes strategies employed to respond to smaller student populations and a limited industrial base, reviewing specific cooperative partnerships between the CCC and local industry; describes partnerships among neighboring campuses; and discusses linking programs to the local economy. The report then provides case studies on the following four programs at rural colleges in the CCC: (1) the Natural Resources and Environmental Majors program at Feather River College, (2) the Lake Tahoe Hospitality Program at Lake Tahoe Community College, (3) the Steam Power Operations Technology Program at Lassen Community College, and (4) the Economic Development Summits at Mendocino College. The final section of the report lists specific steps in identifying local and regional labor market needs and describes the CCC's Labor Market Information and Student Follow-up System, developed to assist the colleges perform labor market analyses. A list of program contact people is included.

O'Rourke, M. "Community College Preservice Training for Paraprofessionals and Related Services Personnel in Rural Kansas." In *Reaching Our Potential: Rural Education in the 90's.* Conference proceedings, Rural Education Symposium, Nashville, Tenn., Mar. 17–20, 1991. 13 pp. (ED 342 580)

This report describes training programs for paraprofessionals to accommodate the rapid growth of special education services in rural Kansas. Developed and implemented by state and local education agencies, the programs are based on the performance competencies established for paraprofessionals, and certification is enforced through the State Department of Special Education. Two federally funded grants have been awarded to the Kansas State Department of Education and the Kansas Association of Community Colleges to provide further support in meeting the training needs. Development of materials are under way to provide skills training at the community college level for special education paraprofessionals who work in integrated, cross-categorical, and early childhood classroom environments. Specific objectives of training programs are addressed. The State of Kansas purchased a licensure and several sets of media material for the First Start Program, which prepares paraprofessionals to care for children with special needs and to assist parents of children with special needs. In addition, many media resources are available for loan through the state department of education to supplement training programs. Facilitators develop and implement programs and recruit trainees in their geographical areas. Interactive television courses are used in the training program.

Starrfield, S. L. "A Longitudinal Cohort Study of Goals, Goal Achievement, and Personal Growth at a Small, Balanced Minority College." *Community Junior College Quarterly of Research and Practice,* 1992, *16* (4), 373–382.

This article describes a longitudinal study of ninety-two new students at South Mountain Community College in Phoenix, Arizona. The study focuses on educational goals and goal strength, grade point average, and postenrollment employment or educational patterns. The author recommends that colleges establish matriculation plans and individual programs of study for students.

West Virginia State Department of Education, Division of Technical and Adult Education. *Sex Equity: Single Parents, Displaced Homemakers, Single Pregnant Women's Projects.* Directory FY–1994. Charleston, Va.: West Virginia State Department of Education, 1994. 80 pp. (ED 368 871)

This directory provides information regarding the sex equity projects and programs in West Virginia that received set-aside Perkins Act funds in fiscal year 1994. Section One describes thirty sex equity programs that are offered through the West Virginia Department of Education. These programs deal with nontraditional jobs for women, tech prep opportunities, teenage pregnancy and parenting, vocational opportunities in rural schools, career awareness, prevocational education, and leadership skills. Section Two discusses eight sex equity projects operated by the West Virginia Community College Division of the State College System of West Virginia. Profiled in Sections Three and Four are a total of forty-two programs offered through the West Virginia Department of Education's Division of Technical and Adult Services (thirty-four programs) and the West Virginia Community College Division (eight programs) to assist single parents, displaced homemakers, and single pregnant women. Among the programs described are those that provide support services, encourage mentoring among female professionals, help women assess career options, and provide special vocational training for nontraditional occupations. Each project or program description includes the name of the school district or agency offering the program, a brief description of the program's objectives and services, and a contact person.

Community Programs

Rural community colleges have implemented outreach and community based programs to address problems of rural life, such as poverty, illiteracy, the need for skilled workers, the lack of health care workers, and high unemployment.

Baldwin, F. "UAB and Community Colleges Link Forces to Train Health Care Professionals." *Appalachia,* 1991, *24* (3), 12–17.

The University of Alabama at Birmingham's Linkage Program focuses on increasing the supply of health care professionals to rural Alabama. Students attend a local community college for one year and the university for another year. Major clinical internships are completed near the students' hometowns. Seventy percent of graduates return to their home areas to work.

Barnett, L. (ed.). *Rural Workplace Literacy: Community College Partnerships.* Washington, D.C.: American Association of Community and Junior Colleges, 1991. 22 pp. (ED 338 300)

In 1990, the American Association of Community and Junior Colleges developed a national workplace literacy demonstration project to raise awareness of the link between local economic development and basic workplace skill performance, and to stimulate a local leadership initiative around a communitywide effort to raise worker performance levels. Ten grants were awarded to the following rural colleges: (1) Columbia College (California), where students from the college and community were recruited to become literacy tutors; (2) Crowder College (Missouri), where adult literacy classes were implemented at work sites; (3) Enterprise State Junior College (Alabama), which coordinated an adult basic education program with six local companies; (4) Genesee Community College (New York), which conducted seminars and workshops for more than 100 farm owners and managers and agribusiness employees; (5) Mount Wachusett Community College (Massachusetts), which developed a flexible, cost-effective tutor training program directed toward unemployed and dislocated workers; (6) New River Community College (Virginia), which provided on-site reading and mathematics classes for workers in the local textile industry who were weak in basic skills; (7) Northeast Texas Community College, which planned and implemented a business-education partnership to enhance workplace literacy in targeted agricultural industries and occupations; (8) Roane State Community College (Tennessee), where a workplace literacy program geared toward unemployed adults and workers with minimal skills was developed; (9) Salish Kootenai College (Montana), which expanded its adult basic education program, developed workplace-related classes, and provided transportation and child care for students on the Flathead Indian Reservation; and (10) Southwestern Oregon Community College, which conducted a workplace literacy project focused on towboat workers, fishermen, apprentices, and underemployed and unemployed adults.

Bishop, J. "Organizational Linkages of the Community College and Recruitment in Literacy Programs." *Community College Review,* 1993, *20* (5), 23–28.

This article advocates interorganizational communication between church, fraternal, and cultural organizations to recruit illiterate adults to rural community colleges. A recruitment strategy at Carteret Community College in North Carolina is discussed. This strategy included research on employee participation in community organizations and informal socials with leaders of underrepresented organizations.

Caldwell, C. A., and Trainer, J. F. "The Campus Role in Enhancing College Participation in a Rural Community." *Community Services Catalyst*, 1991, *21* (1), 3–12.

This article presents a study of low educational interest and participation. Quotes from ethnographic interviews are used to discuss the influences of family, schools, and community on educational decisions. Plans for increasing public awareness and developing new curricula and intervention strategies are described.

Carnes, J. *Northeast Texas Agricultural Literacy Network: A-Lit-NeT: A Rural College Partnership Project. Final Report.* Mount Pleasant, Tex.: Northeast Texas Community College, 1991. 21 pp. (ED 333 917)

In northeast Texas, 47 percent of the adults over the age of twenty-five have not graduated from high school. Area agricultural businesses are rapidly implementing new technologies and quality control measures, both of which require literate and highly trainable workers. To meet these needs, a partnership project was undertaken between Northeast Texas Community College and the Northeast Texas Quality Work Force Planning Committee (Vision-NeT) that focused on enhancing workplace literacy in targeted agricultural industries and occupations. The four goals of the project were to identify industries and occupations with high employment demands; conduct a literacy audit of employees at selected businesses to determine the relationship between workplace literacy and productivity; integrate the results of the literacy audit into the existing Agriculture 2+2 (Tech Prep) and literacy programs; and disseminate the findings of the literacy audit at a Vision-NeT quarterly symposium. Using a labor market information system, three key industries with high projected employment demand were identified (food and kindred products, agricultural production-livestock, and forestry) and a prioritized list of target occupations was developed. A literacy audit of area poultry businesses led to the development of a literacy and occupational skills matrix that could be used to determine the training needs of specific occupations on-site and evaluate and improve occupational education curricula. Finally, as a result of attending the Vision-NeT symposium, Lonestar Steel and a local union entered into a training partnership with Northeast Texas Community College, and currently provide workplace literacy classes to thirty-five employees and members. The following recommendations were given: (1) communication between business and education could be enhanced by avoiding "educationese"; (2) business and education must reach consensus on the definition of basic skills; (3) a more workable taxonomy of basic workplace skills should be developed; (4) where possible, inventories of job duties and tasks should be used to focus literacy audits; (5) community and junior colleges should use a team approach to literacy audits; and (6) in-service training on conducting literacy audits should be provided to community and junior college staff.

Chugh, R. L. *Higher Education and Regional Development: A Compendium of Public Service Activities by Colleges and Universities in Northern New York.* Potsdam, N.Y.: Rural Services Institute, State University of New York, 1992. 229 pp. (ED 354 816)

A study was conducted of the public service programs at the colleges and universities in the Adirondack North Country Association (ANCA) region and how they contribute to the regional development of northern New York State. The study asked the twenty-one institutions in the ANCA area to respond to a survey on various aspects of each institution's public service programs. Twenty institutions responded. The results, summarized in Section One of this report, indicated the following: the institutions regarded public service as very important to their institutional mission; most institutions provide a wide variety of services to meet diverse community needs; local communities are the primary focus for most institutions, followed by the county in which they are located; a high degree of interaction exists between institutions of higher education and their communities; and colleges and universities in the ANCA area significantly contribute to the economic stability of their communities. The second, and largest, section of the report contains campus profiles of the institutions that participated in the study. Each profile contains a description of the institution; descriptions of its significant public service activities and major regional activities; and information on college and community interaction, faculty and staff, students, economic impact, contacts, and conferences, workshops, and noncredit courses.

Enterprise State Junior College and MacArthur State Technical College. *Rural Workplace Literacy Demonstration Project. Final Performance Report.* Opp, Ala.: Enterprise State Junior College and MacArthur State Technical College, 1992. 51 pp. (ED 351 561)

In April 1991, Enterprise State Junior College and MacArthur State Technical College established a rural workplace literacy demonstration project in partnership with adult basic education, seven employers, and a labor organization. The project served 615 people in classes offered at the two colleges, four partner locations, and three additional work sites. The industrial partners and work sites included trailer manufacturers, food processors, metal fabricators, and textile and apparel manufacturers. The project consisted of three main components. The Gateway Component provided remediation for workers with deficiencies in basic skills. The Pathway Component provided needed educational experiences beyond the basic skills and helped workers improve in such areas as problem solving, critical thinking, and work habits. The Linkway Component provided necessary support services to allow workers to participate fully in the project. Indicators of project success were willingness of partners to allow release time and expand employee training, the workers' seeking of additional training after the project's end, and improved worker self-reliance and self-esteem. Appendixes include a needs assessment checklist, a list of available curricula, a sample description of curricula developed for one industry, a twelve-item bibliography, a sample individual education plan, and a report to the National Workplace Literacy Programs.

Esbeck, T. (comp.), and Falcone, L. (ed.). *Economic Development Practices Among Small/Rural Community Colleges*. Washington, D.C.: American Association of Community Colleges, 1993. 110 pp. (ED 356 018) (Paper copies not available from the ERIC Document Reproduction Service; order from American Association of Community Colleges Publications, P.O. Box 1737, Salisbury, MD 21802; $20 [$15 for members].)

In developing this compendium of exemplary economic development practices among small and rural two-year colleges, the American Association of Community Colleges Commission on Small/Rural Community Colleges (CSMCC) sent out a request for program descriptions to all community colleges with less than 3,000 full-time employees or that were self-designated as small or rural. A sample of the best submissions were selected by committee for inclusion in this publication. Following a brief introduction and a listing of CSMCC members, the report presents one-page summaries of 89 economic development programs. The program summaries are grouped into the following categories: (1) efforts in entrepreneurship and new business development, including Bessemer State Technical College's (Alabama) business incubator program and Phillips County Community College's (Arkansas) ethanol production facility study; (2) processes for technology deployment, including Gateway Community Technical College's (Connecticut) automotive cooperative program and Clovis Community College's (New Mexico) instruction via fiber optics program; (3) industrial recruitment and retention efforts, including Alabama Aviation and Technical College's retiree recruitment program and Illinois Central College's economic development consortium; and (4) college relationships with business and industry, including Allen County Community College's (Kansas) robotic installation assistance program and Alexandria Technical College's (Minnesota) center for total quality management training. Each program summary provides the program name, the name of the college, the executive officer, and the college address; the program contact person and his or her telephone number; a summary of exemplary accomplishments; a description of the program and how it was conducted; resource requirements; and a list of key factors in success.

Phillips, W. A. "Developing a Strong Bond Between Education and Local Businesses in Rural Areas." In *Reaching Our Potential: Rural Education in the 90's*. Conference proceedings, Rural Education Symposium, Nashville, Tenn., Mar. 17–20, 1991. 13 pp. (ED 342 558)

This paper describes a Small Business Development Center (SBDC) located at the Central Arizona College. Schools are responsible for assisting in economic development in the small business and business community because industry contributes $22 billion each year toward retraining high school graduates and dropouts in basic education. In Pinal County, Arizona, many students who graduate from or drop out of school stay in the county and take whatever jobs they can find. In 1977, the SBDCs were established nationwide as a method of providing services and assistance to local small business people. The Arizona SBDC Network consists of ten subcenters at community colleges. The services offered to the small businesses in the state are individual counseling, workshops and seminars, a small business library, small business classes, and resource personnel. The Central Arizona College SBDC was established March 1, 1990. The center completed 1990 with 78 counseling cases in the areas of management, financing, accounting, and marketing. Workshops were also offered at times convenient to business people. The SBDC has an advisory committee composed of seven business people and a representative from the State Department of Education and State Community College Board. Businesses are surveyed regarding what job skills they would require of graduates. Business and industry in the community are ready to become involved in the educational process.

Weinberg, M. L., and Burnier, D. "Developing Rural Business Incubators." In G. Waddell (ed.), *Economic and Work Force Development*. New Directions for Community Colleges, no. 75. San Francisco: Jossey-Bass, 1991.

Background on rural entrepreneurship and incubation in the United States is given, with particular focus on rural incubators at community colleges and regional incubation systems. The authors explain how incubators, which provide shared services and business and management assistance for tenant companies, differ from other entrepreneurial development strategies.

Access to Education

The barriers of cost, distance, and scheduling for isolated learners can be alleviated by rural community colleges.

American Association of Community Colleges. *Forgotten Minorities: Rural Americans and the Colleges That Serve Them*. Washington, D.C.: American Association of Community Colleges, 1992. 13 pp. (ED 351 054)

Proactive steps should be taken at the national level to ensure that rural America receives educational and economic opportunities comparable to those provided to the nation's urban regions. This report, by the American Association of Community Colleges' (AACC's) Commission on Small/Rural Community Colleges, details policy and administrative recommendations related to AACC's national agenda priorities. A discussion of rural America's social problems is provided first, dispelling some common misconceptions about rural life and demographics. Next, general policy recommendations are reviewed. These recommendations stem from the commission's suggestion that AACC have one comprehensive concern that affects all Americans: economic viability for the nation through the preservation of existing jobs and the creation of new jobs in the manufacturing, agriculture, service, and information sectors of the economy. The policy and administrative recommendations adopted by the commission in its October 1992 meeting are then provided under the following headings: (1) Advocacy, including specific recommendations concerning economic development, taxes and finance, and general education initiatives in rural areas; (2) Research, including several specific recommendations related to the development and operation of an information center for the community college movement and to the coordination of data collection efforts; and (3) Education and Coordination, offering a recommendation on commission appointments and one on intercommission cooperation. Finally, the commission's planned activities to support AACC's mission in fiscal year 1993 are outlined.

Eschenmann, K. K., and Olinger, P. B. "Barriers Faced by Adult Learners in a Rural Two-Year Community College." *Journal of Studies in Technical Careers,* 1991, *51* (4), 353–363.

A study of ninety-eight adult students was designed to identify the barriers faced by adult students enrolled in two-year degree programs at a community college in a rural area. Problem areas were motivation, family commitments, cost, distance, age, physical limitations, scheduling, and study time.

Hilts, D. J. "Barriers to Adult Learners of an Isolated Northern Community." Master's thesis, University of Oregon, 1991. 47 pp. (ED 340 414)

In 1991, a study was conducted to determine perceptions regarding the deterrents to college attendance among adult learners in an isolated northern community. The study consisted of a survey of forty students at the Fort Nelson campus of Northern Lights College in British Columbia and a follow-up interview with eight of the survey respondents. Subjects for the study were enrolled full time at Northern Lights College during the 1990–91 academic year. The following were major study findings: (1) 57.5 percent of the students surveyed indicated that lack of funding had been a major reason for delaying college entry, and 40 percent indicated that lack of funding could prevent students from achieving college success; (2) lack of self-confidence was cited by 32.5 percent of the respondents as a barrier to entering a college program; (3) over 35 percent of the respondents indicated that the college could help remove barriers by providing information on financial assistance (55 percent), reducing tuition (42.5 percent), providing assistance with day care (40 percent), and providing more useful course offerings (37.5 percent); and (4) the major reasons given for dropping out of college in the past were lack of self-confidence (20 percent), family obligations (17.5 percent), obtaining work (15 percent), and lack of funding (15 percent). Appendixes provide the survey instrument and interview responses.

Illinois Eastern Community Colleges. *Rural Access to Industrial Technologies. Final Report.* Olney: Illinois Eastern Community Colleges, 1991. 238 pp. (ED 346 342)

A pilot academic and vocational Tech Prep program was developed between three rural regional vocational systems and Illinois Eastern Community Colleges to encourage more students to complete a two-year associate degree in industrial technology and obtain employment in industry. Working with three high schools and regional vocational systems and Illinois Eastern Community Colleges, the Tech Prep program influenced approximately 300 faculty. Through a newsletter, meetings, and special events, the program made faculty and administrators more aware of the skill needs of industry, assisted in integrating academic and vocational education, and fostered improved relationships between high schools and the community colleges. Appendixes to the report, which comprise two-thirds of the document, include the following: minutes of meetings of staff and advisory councils, model programs reviewed, manufacturer survey results, the implementation plan, the articulation agreement, project newsletters, survey results from high school vocational classes, and development committee members' Tech Prep ideas.

Rothlisberg, A. P. *Meeting the Competitive Challenge: Encouraging the Use of Community College Library Facilities in Rural, Isolated Northeastern Arizona.* Holbrook, Ariz.: Northland Pioneer College, 1992. 11 pp. (ED 349 971)

This paper describes the approaches taken to improve library service at Northland Pioneer College, a decentralized community college in rural Arizona with learning resource centers at ten locations in Navaho and Apache counties. Three methods of providing instruction for research papers—class tours of learning resource facilities, guest lectures on writing research papers, and a one-credit class on writing research papers—are discussed. Incentives that are arranged in cooperation with local merchants to encourage high-quality student work are described (for example, free pizzas and video rentals), and the effectiveness of such incentives in a rural area is considered. Copies of fliers promoting the incentive program and listing rules for student participation are attached.

Tribal Colleges

Tribal colleges are postsecondary institutions managed by a native tribal government. They tend to be located in rural areas, have small student bodies, and offer programs customized for their local communities and economies.

Ambler, M. "The Wealth of (Indian) Nations: Tribes Are Creating a New Model of Economic Development by Building on Old Strengths." *Tribal College*, 1992, 4 (2), 8–12.

This article assesses economic development on American Indian reservations, focusing on the work of the Coalition for Indian Development, the failure of past economic policies and development efforts, and roles to be played by tribal governments, the federal government, and tribal colleges.

Belgarde, L. "Indian Colleges: A Means to Construct a Viable Indian Identity or a Capitulation to the Dominant Society?" Paper presented at the annual meeting of the American Educational Research Association, New Orleans, Apr. 4–8, 1994. 18 pp. (ED 368 536)

Although tribal colleges were created to provide autonomy in higher education for American Indians, these colleges are dependent on external sources for funds, personnel, and part of their legitimacy. Facing two sets of expectations, administrators of tribal colleges must manage problems experienced by their Indian clientele and adjust institutional routines to the cultural norms of Indian society while also presenting the familiar appearance of a postsecondary educational institution to outside resource providers. Case studies of administration at Turtle Mountain Community College in North Dakota and at Little Big Horn College in Montana demonstrate the effects of funding dependencies on administrative and academic structures. As a consequence of funding dependencies, one site moved toward a more bureaucratized management system over time, while the other reported pressure to do so. Initially, administrators' professional credentials were crucial to the colleges' academic legitimacy. However, as the colleges gained institutional legitimacy, administrators' external roles as professionals became less salient than the bureaucratic structures they had established. Academic structuring showed an opposing trend, as expectations of four-year transfer institutions forced a shift from informal flexible coursework taught by faculty with primarily bachelors degrees to a stable core of courses taught by faculty with advanced degrees. Despite the adoption of formal structures, however, day-to-day practices of both colleges continue to reflect the social patterns of Indian rather than mainstream society.

Brush, L., and others. *Assessment of Training and Housing Needs Within Tribally Con-trolled Postsecondary Vocational Institutions. A Description of Facility and Housing Needs and Five-Year Projections for Meeting Facility and Housing Needs.* Washington, D.C.: Pelavin Associates, 1993. 166 pp. (ED 357 931)

This document contains two reports that assess the facilities and equipment needs of two American Indian technical institutions and suggest five-year plans. United Tribes Technical College in Bismarck, North Dakota, provides one-year and two-year vocational-technical programs to about 280 American Indian students. Because most of the students have low incomes or dependent children, or have never lived off their reservations, the college also provides housing and a variety of support services. Most of the college's buildings are close to 100 years old and require major repairs and renovations. Expansion of enrollment to accommodate students on waiting lists requires construction of additional family housing, dormitories, classrooms, and other facilities. Also needed are computers and training equipment that reflect current practice in occupational areas. The second institution, Crownpoint Institute of Technology in the Navajo Nation in New Mexico, provides one-year technical-vocational programs to about 150 students and continuing education courses to about 200 students. Located in a rural area, Crownpoint Institute of Technology provides virtually all housing for students and faculty. The main building was scheduled for demolition in fall 1992 due to structural problems. Construction needs include replacement structures, additional housing, and facilities for expanding enrollment. Several options for meeting each institution's needs were developed in light of tribal economic development plans and state employment projections. Both of these reports include details on institutional mission and objectives, enrollment, student characteristics, funding, expenditures, and estimated construction costs.

Deloria, V., Jr. "Tribal Colleges and Traditional Knowledge." *Tribal College,* 1993, 5 (2), 31–32.

This article compares the recent advances of Western science to ancient views of Native American tribes. "Advances" such as chaos theory and zoopharmacognosy are indicated to be long-standing elements of Native American traditional knowledge. The author suggests that tribal colleges must assert themselves and become the primary symbols of authority on tribal culture.

McKenzie, J. "Fear and Discovery: An Instructor from the University of North Dakota Reflects on a Summer Spent Teaching at a Tribal College." *Tribal College,* 1993, 5 (1), 29–32.

This article describes an instructor's experience teaching English composition at Turtle Mountain Community College during summer 1990. The difficulties of bicultural education at Indian reservations are explored, and the real meaning of cultural exchanges between American culture and Indian culture is recognized.

Elizabeth Foote is user services coordinator at the ERIC Clearinghouse for Community Colleges, University of California, Los Angeles.

INDEX

Ordering Information

NEW DIRECTIONS FOR COMMUNITY COLLEGES is a series of paperback books that provides expert assistance to help community colleges meet the challenges of their distinctive and expanding educational mission. Books in the series are published quarterly in Spring, Summer, Fall, and Winter and are available for purchase by subscription and individually.

SUBSCRIPTIONS for 1995 cost $49.00 for individuals (a savings of more than 25 percent over single-copy prices) and $72.00 for institutions, agencies, and libraries. Please do not send institutional checks for personal subscriptions. Standing orders are accepted. (For subscriptions outside of North America, add $7.00 for shipping via surface mail or $25.00 for air mail. Orders *must be prepaid* in U.S. dollars by check drawn on a U.S. bank or charged to VISA, MasterCard, or American Express.)

SINGLE COPIES cost $16.95 plus shipping (see below) when payment accompanies order. California, New Jersey, New York, and Washington, D.C., residents please include appropriate sales tax. Canadian residents add GST and any local taxes. Billed orders will be charged shipping and handling. No billed shipments to post office boxes. (Orders from outside North America *must be prepaid* in U.S. dollars by check drawn on a U.S. bank or charged to VISA, MasterCard, or American Express.)

SHIPPING (SINGLE COPIES ONLY): one issue, add $3.50; two issues, add $4.50; three to four issues, add $5.50; five issues, add $6.50; six to eight issues, add $7.50; nine or more issues, add $8.50.

DISCOUNTS FOR QUANTITY ORDERS are available. Please write to the address below for information.

ALL ORDERS must include either the name of an individual or an official purchase order number. Please submit your order as follows:
    Subscriptions: specify series and year subscription is to begin
    Single copies: include individual title code (such as CC82)

MAIL ALL ORDERS TO:
    Jossey-Bass Publishers
    350 Sansome Street
    San Francisco, California 94104-1342

FOR SUBSCRIPTION SALES OUTSIDE OF THE UNITED STATES, contact any international subscription agency or Jossey-Bass directly.

Other Titles Available in the
New Directions for Community Colleges Series
Arthur M. Cohen, Editor-in-Chief
Florence B. Brawer, Associate Editor

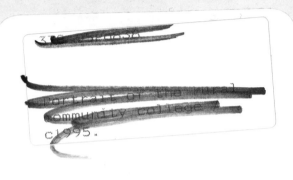

378 ....
.......t of the rural
community college /
c1995.

GAYLORD